the
Cocktail Party

the Cocktail Party

EAT ✳ DRINK ✳ PLAY ✳ RECOVER

MARY GIULIANI

FOREWORD BY MARIO BATALI

BALLANTINE BOOKS
NEW YORK

Copyright © 2015 by Mary Giuliani

Photographs (except as noted below) copyright © 2015 by Adrien Broom

Illustrations copyright © 2015 by Jason O'Malley

Published in the United States by Ballantine Books,
an imprint of Random House,
a division of Penguin Random House LLC, New York.

BALLANTINE and the HOUSE colophon are
registered trademarks of Penguin Random House LLC.

Library of Congress Cataloging-in-Publication Data
Giuliani, Mary.
  The cocktail party : eat-drink-play-recover / Mary Giuliani.
    pages cm
  Includes index.
  ISBN 978-0-553-39350-7 (hardcover : acid-free paper)—
ISBN 978-0-553-39351-4 (eBook)
1. Holiday cooking. 2. Cocktail parties. 3. Cocktails. I. Title.
  TX739.G58 2015
  641.87'4—dc23
                    2015020103

Printed in China on acid-free paper

randomhousebooks.com

9 8 7 6 5 4 3 2 1

First Edition

Book design by Jason O'Malley
Photographs on pages xviii, xix, 2, and 160–61 by Jonny Valiant

*To Gala Lee
my greatest party . . .*

"I CHOOSE TO START WITH COCKTAILS BECAUSE NO GREAT STORY EVER STARTED WITH A SALAD."

—*Amelie Laurent*

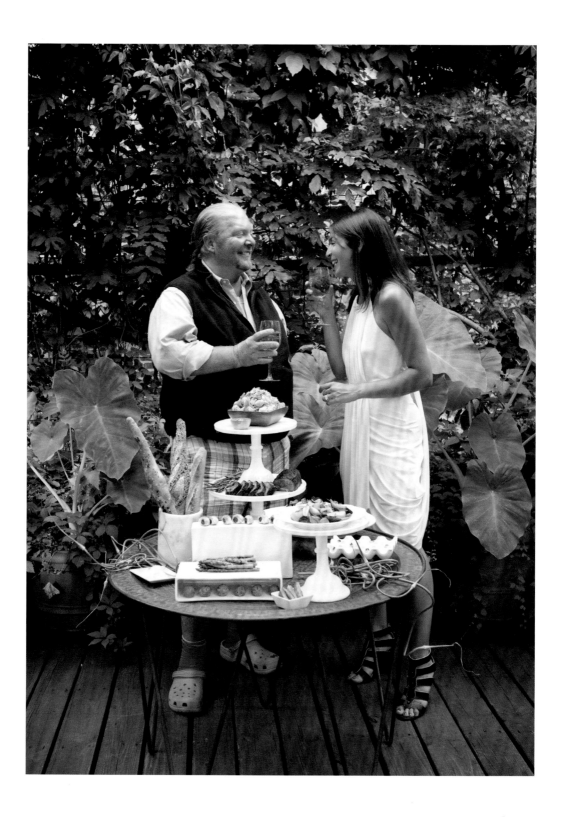

The Cocktail Party, Mary G's ingenious book on creating joyous food and poetically festive events, is mouthwateringly beautiful and, most of all, easy, much like Mary herself. There are times when I go to a party and realize that the food is far more interesting and delectable than most of the guests, and far more savory and provocative than the modern "art" in the foyer. Most often in NYC, it happens at a party catered by Mary Giuliani and her covey of enchanted chefs and wickedly talented service staff. Mary definitely puts the FU in fun and the yum in delicious and this remarkably sweet, spicy, and tangy book captures all of the magnificent simplicity of Mary's food and at least half of her incredible wit, passion, and joy for something done deliciously and perfectly right. This is a handbook for living well and appreciating life with joyous abandon.

—MARIO BATALI

Contents

INTRODUCTION

ALL THE WORLD'S A STAGE; MY STAGE IS YOUR TABLE

When I was a little girl, my favorite game to play with my mother was What Do You Want to Be? She would sit me on her lap, look me in the eyes, and ask me this all-important question, "Mary, what do you want to BE?" If my wish was to be a princess, she would gently press her finger against my lips, and poof! I had lipstick. A slight brush of my head and there was my tiara, sprinkles of magic dust followed, and *ta-da* . . . I was a princess.

We must have played this game hundreds of times. I was everyone from a zookeeper to Charo from *The Love Boat*. But not once, even growing up in a family whose lives revolved around food and parties, did I look up and say, "Mommy, I want to be a caterer."

Please keep in mind this was LONG before the days when that magical chef with the orange Crocs showed up; when people ordered food to eat rather than to Instagram. WAY before vodka was infused with bacon, and before tacos were gourmet, when the party-throwing world was a Pinterest-pressure-free zone. This was more of the "I'm gonna work in the food industry because I'm on parole" kind of times.

After graduating from Georgetown University, I figured it was no more games, I actually did have to figure out what I wanted to be for real this time. I'd set my sights on being an actress, so I worked as a coat check girl at Nobu (where I was fired and given the honor of being called "the most inconsistent, unreliable employee" they'd ever had), auditioned for James Lipton for a coveted spot at The

Actors Studio (he basically laughed me off the stage), worked for an entertainment agency (where I was fired for sending in my head shot for the role of Meadow Soprano instead of one of the actress I was *supposed* to be representing), dabbled in fund-raising, took jazz dance classes, went to grad school for a semester, and played a terrorist in an off-off-off Broadway play.

After a string of short-lived jobs, and not much success in the acting world (unless you consider being an extra in Whit Stillman's *The Last Days of Disco* success), I randomly answered an ad in the *New York Times* that listed "Upscale boutique catering firm seeks temporary employee to work with art, fashion, and entertainment clients."

I was drawn to "entertainment" and "temporary." A week later, I began my new role as Mary Giuliani, Catering Sales Representative.

When I walked into the office of New York's DM Cuisine, I knew very little about table settings, samovars (look that one up), steps of service, or how to properly spell the word *hors d'oeuvre*. At the time, my kitchen cabinets at home contained a fondue pot, six mismatched martini glasses, and my mom's M-O-M mug.

But, little did I know that this job, which I took with no greater hopes than to be able to pay my cable bill, would be my ticket to a world I could only have imagined entering, with a trusty pig in a blanket as my admission ticket!

For the first time, it all made sense: I was good at throwing parties, loved working creatively with food and drinks, and found that my greatest joy came from

stepping back and watching our clients enjoy themselves at the parties I was overseeing, which were like mini theatrical performances. And while Robert De Niro was never gonna hand me that Oscar, I traded in that dream for another and offered him a tray of crab cakes instead.

But wait, don't think that this revelation came easily or overnight. I would spend many years working harder than I'd ever thought possible, under the guidance of a most talented catering chef, who would also turn out to become one of my biggest mentors, Daniel Mattrocce.

If this were a movie, this part of my life would be the visual montage moment. You know what I'm talking about. It's the best part of the movie! The music speeds up, all starts to go well for the character—she starts with flour in her hair and a burnt chicken, and by the end of that one song she has a new haircut, a great new outfit, is walking confidently . . . and that chicken? It finally comes out of the oven perfectly!

Daniel was constantly showing me how hard this business and this career choice was going to be. Many times he reminded me why I should pack up my Luccis and go (I couldn't afford Gucci, so my mom bought me a pair of soap star Susan Lucci's shoes from QVC . . . I wore them all the time). But his challenges only made me want to rise to the occasion (literally) even more.

At DM, I did everything from answer the phones, to book staff, clean the office (not well), order rentals, conceptualize menus and party ideas, and even help Daniel in the kitchen (a few times at 3:30 a.m. for an early-morning breakfast). I was not cooking the food, but I was coming up with creative menu ideas. Food magazines were where I was told to find ideas (remember, this was early-Internet), but I began to also seek inspiration from cult films, art, fashion, and music.

Another thing exciting about this new job was that no two days were the same. I was uptown, downtown, sometimes two or three times on the same day. I was meeting people from all walks of life: artists, celebrities, socialites, musicians, business tycoons, and they trusted ME(!?) with their special occasion. It was the most amazing front-row ticket to some of the best lives in town. Hungry and thirsty (sometimes literally) to take it all in and learn as much as I could, I did.

A typical week would take me to the greenroom of the New York City Ballet, the private sales gallery at Christie's Auction House, where Elizabeth Taylor and her dog were the guests of honor, Kevin Klein's apartment while he was preparing for the role of Cole Porter, a Breast Cancer Awareness luncheon, and a billionaire's yacht.

But it wasn't just the fancy people or places that lit up my new world, it was the kind hippie booker that would sage the office after every bad party, the chefs and sous chefs (all characters) working in the kitchen, my first trip to the flower market at 4 a.m., the gangster-type ice delivery man who would propose marriage to me every time I placed an order, the fishmongers, you name it . . . so many new people and places, so many lessons to learn. I would return to my small studio apartment each night (usually with a Gray's Papaya hot dog in my hand) physically and mentally exhausted, but filled with something I'd never felt before—inspiration.

Keep in mind it wasn't all glamorous. There were also early mornings and late nights, stressful phone calls, heart-stopping event mistakes (I once ran fifteen blocks in high heels because I forgot to order dishes for a dinner!!! Thank you, Crate & Barrel), long hours, and bloody feet! I was working harder than I'd ever imagined I'd work in my life (and for a girl who previously would often get caught taking naps under her desk, this was a big deal), but the difference was, I started to realize that I was doing what I loved and that dreams could change.

And then the realization set in that for the first time, after being gifted with all the amazing glimpses my career had allowed me, I did not aspire to be anyone else but me! I wanted to be exactly what I was— "their caterer"—because nothing brought me more joy than a happy smile or a sincere thank-you at the end of a party. I was *hooked*.

I started to think about food and beverage as an extension of my clients, what they were looking to promote, what they wanted to say, and I was so excited to go off on my own and express these thoughts creatively with my unique food and beverage ideas. The sky was the limit. As I came into my own in the catering world and developed all these ideas for my clients, I knew that I would eventually leave my mentor and devote my energy to growing my own business.

In March of 2005, my husband, Ryan, and I liquidated our savings account (less than $5,000) and Mary Giuliani Catering & Events was born in the living room of our one-bedroom apartment. I hand-glued our business cards, we took turns using our one computer that took up most of our living room, set up a phone line, and hoped it would ring.

Thankfully it did! Good luck meeting good timing was how we got our first big gig, when a friend called saying that he had TEN parties in one week for the upcoming Tribeca Film Festival and needed a caterer. Without knowing if we could even do it, I said yes and made sure that we did! Thanks to my dad for teaching me, "Never say 'I can't,' rather, say 'I'll try!'"

Ten parties, seven sleepless nights, 1,500-plus happy customers, and Mary

Giuliani Catering & Events quickly grew from an idea into a real company!

From there, we moved to a real office, and added real employees. People who shared the same love of food and entertaining as we did, and it was SO exciting.

I felt very strongly that we were being given the opportunity to work with the finest names in art, fashion, and entertainment and it was up to us to make sure that we never took that gift for granted and constantly tried to source the best food and drink experiences for our clients. And I made the decision early on that even though the clients were fancy, our attitudes were going to be anything but.

I needed to stay true to who I was and what I liked about food and gathering. I was not a superfoodie, and it was important to me that the food experience felt inspired, welcoming, and like going home. The experience would be unique, whimsical, comfortable, and approachable, with nostalgic warmth. We would seek food inspiration from unlikely places. And while some people thought serving mini grilled cheese and tiny hamburgers would never work for the A-list of the A-listers, Mary Giuliani waiters could be found serving just that up and down the chicest stores and residences on Madison and Fifth Avenues.

Within our first year of business, we did parties for *InStyle, Vogue,* The Rolling Stones, and even *Harry Potter*!!! You should know I was so petrified that our young company could pull off such a large event (the *Harry Potter* movie premiere) that I spent half of the party hiding in a bathroom stall praying (I'm not kidding).

When I look back and think about how this all happened, I'm not really sure. I think luck, timing, a keen eye for talented chefs, hardworking waiters, passionate planners, and the fact that my husband and I were

growing this together during a fabulous food boom had lots to do with it. I think pushing the envelope and dancing to the beat of my own drum by breaking entertaining norms was a refreshing new perspective in the New York catering scene, so the greater the response to a new tray or food concept, the more I was inspired to get really creative and dig deep for more new and exciting ideas and concepts.

Mostly, though, I think it's because I'm motivated purely by making people happy. I served (and still do serve) straight from my heart, to both my clients and my employees. And even after more than five thousand parties, my company receiving prestigious awards, and appearing in magazines and TV, working for some of my biggest idols, collaborating with Mario Batali, and cooking grilled cheese with the Barefoot Contessa, I'm still very much that young girl who arrived in Daniel's kitchen in her Luccis. I remain grateful to be in the game, grateful that I get to do what I love, and especially grateful for every entry to a new place, brought to me via a tray of pigs in a blanket.

This year, Mary Giuliani Catering & Events will celebrate its tenth year in business, Ryan is now off pursuing his dreams (opening a hotel and restaurant), we have fifteen full-time employees and two amazing business partners, and I'm still happy to work in the home I helped build with a dream.

So after all this pressure, and luckily a touch of success, what do I do for fun? Well, after a long week of throwing parties in New York City for a living, you'd think the last thing I'd wanna do on the weekend is entertain at home. But downtime for me means throwing creative gatherings at my Hudson Valley home (Woodstock, New York, to be exact), replete with themes, party favors, décor, handcrafted drinks, and menus that are big on fun and flavor.

Talk about doing what you love!? These parties give me an opportunity to recharge my creative juices and try out new ideas on a cadre of wonderful friends, family, and neighbors.

So what's next?

My next new dream is to be welcomed into *your home,* as your new pal and trusted source for throwing your own hassle-free parties. The same philosophy that I apply to serving my clients now goes for you. It doesn't need to be fancy or difficult to be amazing and memorable, so, in the pages that follow, I wish to share with you all that I learned from years of victories (many), mistakes (many), and the *how did I get into this party?* moments. The food may be small, but the stories I'll share will be big.

I'd love to encourage you to shake things up (both on your table and in your glass), and offer you a reminder that there is no such thing as a "perfect life" or a "perfect party." I'm going to show you my trusty, go-to tricks that will save you from party stress and at the same time get you to kick off your shoes, turn up the music, and dance around your kitchen before your guests arrive.

Do you have to be a chef to use this book?? *Not at all!* I am *not* a chef. I am just someone who deeply loves gathering people and providing them with great food, drinks, and memories. And if you love that too, then you already have the greatest ingredient for your next party.

I hope that in reading *The Cocktail Party* you'll feel like you have a pal on the inside who wants to see you succeed. That you will take away a few key ideas and approaches, including that parties should always make people laugh, that mini grilled cheese sandwiches are never a bad idea, that mac and cheese *can* be served on a Ferris wheel, and most important, that even if you don't know what you want to be when you grow up (no matter how old you are), your dreams can come true . . . including the ones you didn't even know you had.

Love,
Mary

WHY COCKTAIL PARTIES?

I am named after both of my grandmothers, Mary and Lucille. I often joke that I am the perfect "mixed cocktail" of both of these women.

Mary (my mom's mom) was a loving, traditional housewife who cared for her children, kept a beautiful home, and cooked delicious meals for her family every night (she also created an amazing cook, my mom . . . who taught me all I know).

Lucille (my dad's mom) was a maverick business owner, who in the 1950s left the kitchen to pioneer in the fairly undiscovered beach town of Montauk, New York. During her time there, she owned and operated several successful hotels and became known as the hostess with the mostess, welcoming thousands of tourists to her hotels each summer. And her party of choice . . . was, of course, the Cocktail Party.

On "party nights" in Montauk, my sister and I would be put to bed in our hotel

rooms on the property and instructed not to go to Grandma Lucille's house, as it was for "adults only." My curiosity would often get the best of me and I would end up sneaking into her party to scope out the action. Knowing I needed to remain undercover, I would hide under a cocktail table, while trays of deviled eggs and martinis were passed around the room and the aroma of salt water and wafts of cigarette smoke filled the air.

To Lucille, a successful cocktail party meant a diverse guest list. So, there were fishermen clinking glasses with politicians, artists breaking bread with handymen and celebrities, even one time a priest and a rabbi (and no, this is not the setup for a joke). And there she was, in the center of it all, making sure glasses were filled, canapés were on the right-sized trays, and the stories being told were big.

I usually got away with my little visits unnoticed, but one night, Grandma Lucille spotted my small foot peeking out from under the tablecloth, and instead of ratting me out to my parents, she gave me a wink and pushed my feet back under the table, to help conceal my hiding spot. I think she enjoyed that I wanted in on the scene.

I guess you could say that moment was a defining one for me. I still feel like that little girl today when peeking in at my own parties and watching guests enjoy themselves, and although I've catered breakfasts, dinners, weddings, film premieres, divorce parties, dog birthdays, art gallery openings, store openings, yacht launchings, funerals, film shoots, product launches, and more, the Cocktail Party remains my absolute favorite way to entertain!

There is something wonderfully retro and nostalgic about the words *cocktail party*. They elicit images of women in hostess pajamas smoking cigarettes while making Jell-O and men in natty suits filling their glasses with Scotch and telling jokes. In fact, the 1960s (the decade that speaks to me the most) was really the first time hosts used food and beverages as extensions of their personal styles. I also like the "rules" of a classic Cocktail Party, as passed down from all those wonderful hostesses of the '50s and '60s, although really, by their very nature, there are no real rules. But here goes. . . .

COCKTAIL PARTIES GENERALLY HAVE START AND END TIMES. THEY ARE OFTEN NO LONGER THAN TWO TO THREE HOURS.

COCKTAIL PARTIES ARE MOSTLY INFORMAL AND FUN, FOCUSED AROUND CONVERSATION AND DRINKING.

COCKTAIL PARTIES FEATURE HORS D'OEUVRES, WHICH IN MY OPINION ARE THE PERFECT FOOD.

COCKTAIL PARTY ENTERTAINING ALLOWS FOR WHIMSICAL AND INVENTIVE FOOD DISPLAY. COCKTAIL PARTIES AND STORYTELLING GO VERY WELL TOGETHER AND I THINK YOU'LL DEDUCE BY THE END OF THIS BOOK THAT NO ONE LOVES A GOOD STORY MORE THAN I.

So to sum that all up, the cocktail party is a wonderful opportunity for the home entertainer to show off his or her skills (or lack thereof) in a condensed amount of time with minimal expectations of anything beyond snack food and stiff cocktails.

Years ago (pre–*Mad Men*), I became obsessed with reinventing the cocktail party for the modern host because I saw how wonderfully people responded to small bites and interactive food stations. As life has gotten busier and entertaining options have gotten more elaborate, it can sometimes be daunting to pull it all off perfectly. Cocktail parties are efficient, creative, and a great way to entertain.

HOW TO USE THIS BOOK

The Cocktail Party formula can be applied not just to the traditional 6 to 8 p.m. party hours, but can be used to execute perfect planning for morning, noon, and late-evening parties as well. Occasions featured in this book range from daytime game watching to afternoon showers to midnight breakfasts.

You can use the ideas from this book to inspire any party. Start with an occasion. You got a promotion. A friend had a baby. The seasons are changing. Your neighbor just got out of jail (told you I love a good story!).

The occasion is then broken into four parts: EAT, DRINK, PLAY, RECOVER

EAT
(SMALL BITES, SMALL SWEETS, AND SNACKTIVITIES)

Hors d'oeuvres, or small bites, rose in popularity in the 1960s, largely due to the rise in Americans' consumption of cocktails and the need for something to soak up all the booze! Pretty good reason to fall in love quickly with this new food concept.

I fell in love with hors d'oeuvres, particularly the pig in a blanket, while attending more than 175 bar and bat mitzvahs during my early teen years. Since I was often the only Italian girl at these shindigs (looking like Ralph Macchio in a pink poufy dress), that tray of buttery, salty, crispy, and tangy hot dogs would often become my companion for the duration of the party.

Perhaps my greatest hors d'oeuvre revelation came when I started working in catering and saw that these mini bites of food made people happy, pure and simple. They are the most anticipated part of a party menu; they are pretty; they are unique; they're like eating small bites of art. Night after night, I saw the trays leave the kitchen, enter the party, and bring smiles. And as a caterer who lives to see people happy, this was all I needed to become an hors d'oeuvre/small bite devotee.

But when I entered the world of catering, hors d'oeuvres were often time-consuming and hard to make: fancy, savory, precious little pastries. So I started to think about all the comfort foods that I loved and frequently ate, like mac and cheese, hot dogs, grilled cheese, cheese steaks, et cetera, and thought, "Hey, why not shrink these popular items into hors d'oeuvre size?" and, *voilà* . . . people got even happier at our parties.

What I loved most about the new combo of comfort and elegance was that the ingredients and preparation became more simple, so that you didn't need to be a Cordon Bleu–trained chef to make hors d'oeuvres. In order to master these perfect bites, you, like me, could just be a home cook with a passion for entertaining.

So, for each occasion, recipes will be provided for two homemade hors d'oeuvres and two homemade mini sweets for you to master. By the end of the book, you'll have lots of unique small bites to impress your party pals.

SMALL SWEETS One pie is great, but how about two or three small bites of three different pies? I'm a big fan of variety in my sweets—and, I can assure you, so are your guests! I'll show you a few ways to dazzle with variety. Remember, you only get one chance to make a *last* impression. So make sure your sweets are memorable.

Now let's discuss *Snacktivities*.

One night, my pal Adrien and I were discussing how much we loved customizing food. I told her about our catering company's hugely popular mac and cheese bar, where you could top your mac with things like bacon, jalapeños, and truffle oil. I then told her about our mozzarella bar, where you could add things like pancetta, roasted tomatoes, and balsamic caviar to what would otherwise be an ordinary (albeit delicious) piece of cheese. "It's like a snacktivity!" she blurted out. She had created *the best* new word for what has been traditionally called a "buffet" or "food" bar. From that point on, I made sure that all my home entertaining offered my guests some type of snacktivity bar, composed mostly of store-bought foods. Snacktivities are *all* about the presentation.

So each chapter will also have two wonderful food snacktivity displays that can be a combination of store-bought items uniquely displayed to get you those party WOWs.

DRINK

Not much to say here other than if you picked up this book, chances are you, too, are a lover of LARGE cocktails. And if you are a nervous host at all, I'll tell you now that the combination of small bites and big drinks already brings you more than halfway toward party perfection. The big drinks in this book will be both large in flavor and creativity—and are also offered in large quantities so your guests can help

themselves, leaving you more time to enjoy the night. Every drink recipe in the book is meant to be poured into a punch bowl, drink dispenser (see suggested ones in the Party Closet & Tools section, page xxvi), large pitchers, a bucket, or any vessel that can hold a batch of cocktails to serve eight to ten guests.

PLAY

Play applies to all the stuff we're gonna do to make your party special . . . play with your dishes, your glasses, theme, table linens, furniture, location, music, and party games. I'll load you up with some unique ways to rethink the average household items you already own and use, or those collecting dust in your cabinets . . . stuff that will hopefully give you a new or inspired groove for your parties.

And because I'm a huge fan of the pre-guest-arrival party ritual of dancing around your house while getting ready, I'll give you Party Prep Playlists that will help you do just that!

RECOVER

If you're anything like me and helped yourself to a few too many grapefruit-jalapeño margaritas, you'll need some advice or tips on how to feel a little bit better the next day. I'm here to help you see things a little more clearly the next day by offering some tips for recovery, cleaning, restocking, and recharging.

BIG STORIES

And finally, no cocktail party is complete without a few good stories, so I'm happy to share with you some fun ones from my childhood and my office—inside and outside (sometimes from the bushes) the party.

PARTY CALCULATOR

**Math was never my strongest subject,
so I'm going to keep this really simple for you.**

....

The whole book is broken down into what you will need for a two-hour party for ten guests. If you are having more guests or if the party will last longer, simply multiply the quantities based on the number of guests and number of hours.

Some general Cocktail Party rules of thumb:

HORS D'OEUVRES
You should have 4 or 5 pieces of each item you are serving per person, per hour of party.

Each chapter has 4 small bites (2 savory, 2 sweet) making quantities of 24 pieces per item . . . therefore, each chapter yields 96 pieces of food, completing the equation.

SNACKTIVITIES
There is no exact math for this one . . . but if you follow my blueprints, I promise you'll have enough to get you through the 2 to 3 hours. Again, if your party is longer, or you're having more than 8 to 12 guests, up your quantities or get a bigger table.

DRINKS
More math . . . Oy vey!

The general rule is that guests will have 2 drinks during the first hour (to get those stories coming) and then 1 drink for every hour that follows.

Glasses . . . if you're having 10 guests, have 20 glasses. Always double the number of guests to get the correct number of glasses.

1 bottle of wine fills about 7 glasses of wine.

1 bottle of champagne (or prosecco or sparkling wine) fills 6 champagne flutes.

1 bottle of hard alcohol makes about 12 cocktails.

ANATOMY of a COCKTAIL PARTY

2 hours   *10 people*   = PARTY

SMALL BITES

savory

24

24

4-5 per person / hr

sweet

24

24

DRINKS

2 drinks per person 1st hr,
1 drink every hour after

wine
7 glasses / bottle

6 flutes / bottle
champagne

spirits
12 cocktails / bottle

$$\frac{\text{\# of guests} \times 2}{= \text{\# of glasses}}$$

PARTY CLOSET & TOOLS

Just because the food that we're preparing looks so adorably tiny and precious doesn't mean the prep work has to be. Here's what you need to be perfectly "party trained" and ready for action at the drop of a toothpick! I like to keep these items on hand in my pantry and by my bar.

....

- *Cookie cutters*

- *Pizza cutter*

- *Mini muffin pans*

- *Mini ice scream scoop (25mm). The mini ice cream scoop is a very important "caterer's shortcut"; we will use this lots in our recipes.*

- *Sharp knives*

- *Cutting board*

- *Warming tray (Dust off your mother's or buy a new one. There are a zillion inexpensive retro ones for sale on eBay or Etsy.)*

- *Small bowls for dips and snacktivity toppings (I like white or clear to show off what's inside, but it's your party; feel free to use what you like best.)*

- *Toothpicks, umbrellas, mini forks, whatever floats your boat, we'll discuss.*

- *Cocktail napkins, small plates (Everything we're serving can go on a small plate or cocktail napkin. This is not a large-plate cookbook.)*

- *Two boxes frozen pigs in a blanket . . . just in case*

- *Good mixed nuts*

- *Cocktail shaker and strainer*

- *Ice tub and ice scoop*

- *Garnish bowls for your lemon and lime wedges (oh, and lemons and limes)*

- *Drink dispensers (I will use this term often in the drink recipes.) These are vessels that can hold beverages: pitchers, punch bowls, beverage dispensers for juices and mixers. (All the drink recipes will be shown in large-batch quantities, so you don't have to play bartender and hostess.)*

- *All-purpose glasses: tumblers, rocks, pilsner, shot, martini . . . (I don't love wineglasses or flutes, but if you do, use 'em. I prefer a rocks glass for wine.) These can be glass or acrylic or, if you've got the room and like to entertain outside, a set of each. For me, a set is twelve of each, but stock what you know you'll use again and again.*

- *Wine opener and stopper, champagne stopper*

- *One chilled / temperature-appropriate bottle of your fave red, white, or sparkling wine*

- *Sparkling water*

- *Grapefruit juice (my go-to mixer)*

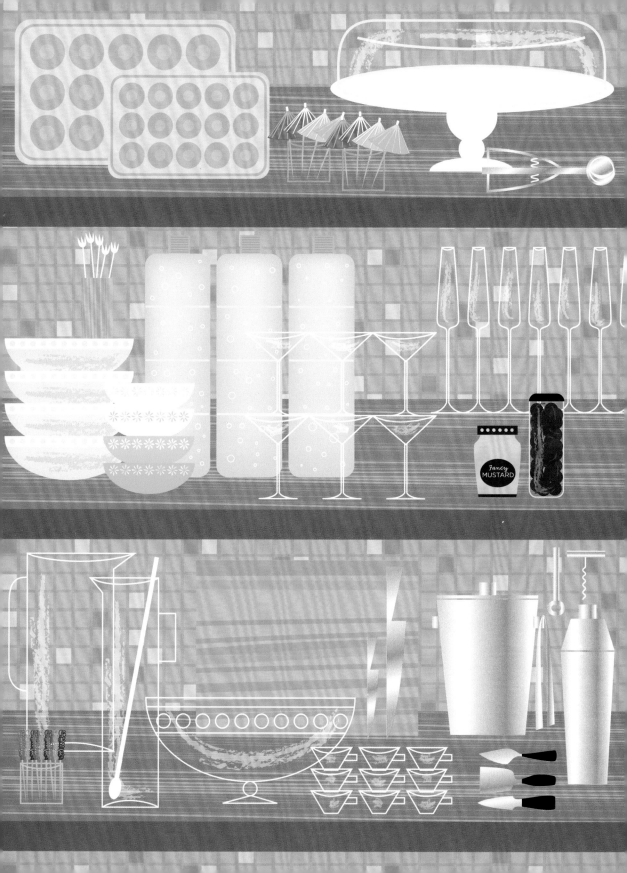

the Cocktail Party ™

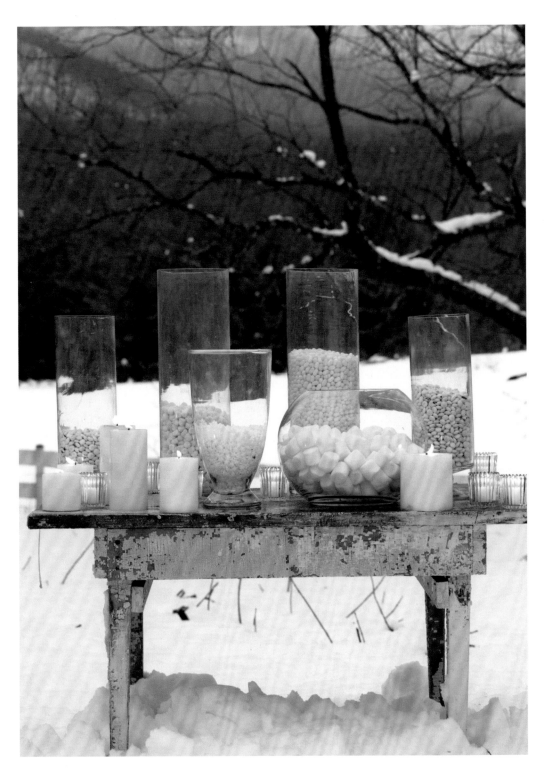

Holidays and Cocktail Parties—

HOW TO GET IT RIGHT EVERY TIME!

So while this book is laid out according to various occasions that fall throughout the year (some common, some uncommon), there is no busier time on the cocktail party calendar than the fall/winter holidays. And while the recipes, flavors, décor, and themes may change for each of these gatherings, if you stick to these few simple rules during the holiday season, you'll come off looking like a pro each and every time.

EAT

The parties in this book are designed to work because you can do most of the preparation in advance of your guests arriving. For example, the night before your event is a great time to get most of your cooking done. All the small bites recipes provided in this book can be prepared in advance, either the night before or the morning of, and then refrigerated and reheated, freeing up time to pull off your "day of" duties.

Also pull out all of your platters, trays, silver or plasticware, dishes, etc. For the Snacktivities portion of the party (which is comprised mostly of store-bought items), lay out all the bowls and platters beforehand, and place the still packaged items you bought onto the designated serving dishes to see a mock set-up. This will eliminate any excessive searching for "just the right bowl" as guests are walking through the door, and will give you complete peace of mind to know the whole party is organized. For me, if I go to bed seeing it all laid out . . . I'm already that much calmer the next day.

Food themes are helpful to keeping your party cohesive. So don't serve a Mexican bean dip next to a tray of mini pizzas. If

you're going with the bean dip, how about some taquitos or mini quesadillas? This will also help you choose your drink. Serving Mexican fare? Offer tequila-based cocktails. Italian fare? Then wine and a Campari cocktail. Asian fare? Sake . . . you get it.

When it comes to how much food to serve, remember, we're talking a two- to three-hour party MAX so don't feel like you have to put out tons of food. Cocktail party entertaining means nibbles and cocktails, NOT a formal meal. If the words "Cocktail Party" appear on your invite, no one will expect dinner, even for a Thanksgiving-themed cocktail party, I promise you.

For your guests' ease and your own, make sure everything you are serving requires no more than one small plate, one fork, and one cocktail napkin. If something requires anything larger than that, don't serve it. Who needs the hassle?

Keep the cheese tray separate. Give it the respect it deserves. Cheese can go with any themed-cuisine party but works best if you keep it separate. And as with food, you can tie in appropriate crackers or biscuits or bread. There's a world of difference between rice crackers, semolina breadsticks, and hearty fruit and nut crisps. Branch out and get creative. A great cheese tray, by the way, is always appealing, even to the pickiest eater.

Spread out your party, if you can. Serve your small bites in the kitchen, Snacktivities in the living room, and dessert near the fireplace or in the kitchen. Guests like to move around. If you're entertaining in one room (like I did for years in my studio apartment), think about something fun you can do to switch it up. Clean out a closet and make it your bar, fill up your bathtub with ice and fill it with bottles. Coffee tables, end tables, credenzas, even your bed (properly covered—and made!) can be used for food and drink display. Get creative.

Have fun with your displays and improvise as needed. If you run low on serving platters or trays, serving out of and on top of pots and pans is a good alternative. They can also make great snacktivity display stands. One year I served a bunch of brownies on my pots, which I had turned upside down; it gave new meaning to the words *pot brownies*!

DRINK

Holidays are not the time to show off your entire dusty bottle collection. Keep your bar simple. All you need is red and white wine, one specialty cocktail, soda, and sparkling water. DONE.

Pre-batch your drinks (loads of ideas in this book) so that you're not bartending all night.

Make sure you have enough glassware, and remember there is nothing wrong with using disposables.

If you have an icemaker, start a few days before, making and bagging extra ice. If you don't, then make sure you buy enough to last the night. The general rule of thumb on this is 6 to 8 ounces of ice per guest plus more

for chilling wine. Ice for drinks can be set out fifteen minutes before your guests arrive, around the same time you're pouring yourself your second cocktail. Did I mention that you should have your first an hour before that?

Don't forget your garnishes. My rule of thumb is six limes and six lemons for every party and then anything fun or fancy if you want to add in. Grapefruit is a nice drink garnish in lieu of lemons.

PLAY

Two hours prior to your guests' arrival, begin your pre-party ritual. Blast that party prep playlist and have some fun while you prepare your party environment. The more love and fun that goes into the planning, the more fun and love your guests will feel. No one wants to show up and find a frazzled and exhausted host (that's why you prepped in advance).

Two hours prior is also a great time to start chilling wine (although you really only need 45 minutes—but again—a prepared host is a happy host!).

Walk through your party from start to finish from the perspective of your guests.

Arrival:

Where will coats go? On the bed or on a rack outside the apartment? Make sure you think about this before and designate an area.

Now, where's the bar? Make sure you place the bar in the most visible location from the party entry. The food can be placed nearly anywhere, but the bar must be visible.

Bathrooms Did you remember to place a nice votive candle and some extra hand towels or at least one clean cotton towel?

Introduce your guests with something they can talk about when you have to walk away and get the door:

"Cindy, meet Ryan. Ryan just moved to New York from Chicago and Cindy grew up in Chicago."

BAM, they are now chatting away about how much they love the new Eataly.

Your snacktivity table should also be set two hours prior; however, save things like breads and lids off dips (especially guac) until about a half hour prior. Quick tip: If your guac starts to turn brown, either squeeze a lime in it and mix or cover with a dollop of sour cream. Also, a damp paper towel over your breads and crudités will help those items remain fresh.

Keep an eye on your party clock. It's the holidays, so at around 2½ hours, start thinking about how you're going to wrap up this baby. Dessert is the best way to send that message. In addition to dessert, I often serve black coffee in espresso cups; it also sends a little hint that this party is winding down.

Send your guests home with something to remember the night. A bag of candy, a warm cup of hot chocolate in a to-go cup, two bagels and some cream cheese for the next morning in a brown paper bag . . . your kids. Whatever.

RECOVER

There are a bunch of things you can do to make sure your cleanup goes quickly and smoothly and it starts with a clean house and kitchen before your guests arrive. I am crazy about everything being in order prior to my guests' arrival, so that all I have to do is clean up the party, rather than every square inch of space. My dishwasher is *always* empty before my party starts and there are always multiple trash bags in my garbage can on party nights.

Make sure you have containers or to-go wares on hand. I always offer my guests the option to take a little something home. The more they take home, the less I have to clean up and put away.

Clean up the same night. The most important piece of wisdom I can impart to you is CLEANING UP WITH A BUZZ IS MUCH BETTER THAN WITH A HANGOVER. Use that pre-party playlist again, crank up those tunes, and get cleaning. Do NOT allow yourself to go to sleep with a dirty house. You'll thank yourself in the morning!

CHAPTER 1

Thanksgiving

EAT

Turkey with Cranberry on
Mini Pumpkin Muffins

Mashed Potato Popovers with Mozzarella

Mini Pecan & Rosemary Pies

Mini Pumpkin-Caramel Brownies

DRINK

Tipsy Turkey Martini

Cider House Rules

PLAY

How to Set a Less Is More Bar

Soup Sipping Station

Mini Pie / Brownie Stand

RECOVER

Hangover Kit Assembly

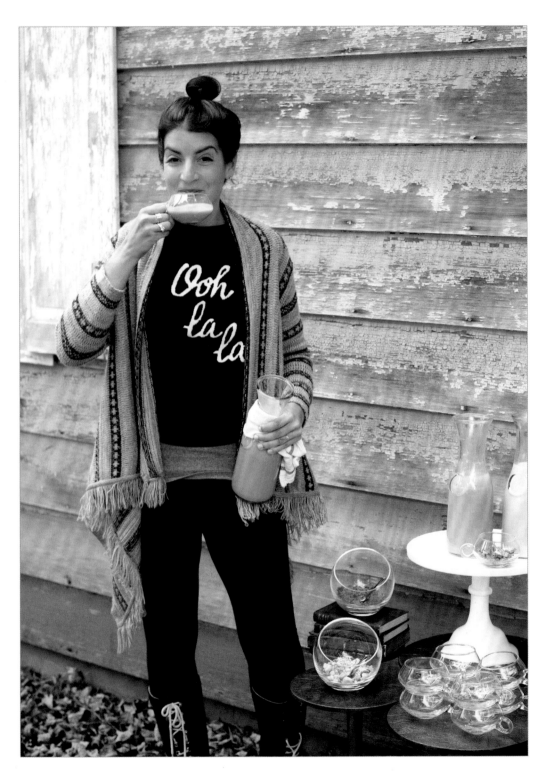

To be perfectly honest, I've only catered *one* Thanksgiving in my entire career, and it was a disaster (we'll get to that story shortly). However, it taught me two very important things about Thanksgiving entertaining: First, less is more, something you never hear when it comes to Thanksgiving. Second, Thanksgiving should be spent with family, friends, or loved ones, *not* with a caterer. If you cringe thinking about a long, drawn-out meal with heated family discussions around the dinner table, then a Cocktail Party Thanksgiving is perfect for you, since there's no dining room table required for it. If this concept scares you completely and entertaining without sitting at a table just will not cut it for your Thanksgiving gathering, then use this party as a fun night of thanks with your pals, pre-Thanksgiving recipe testing, or a gratitude party. While these recipes and ideas are great for Thanksgiving, they can also serve as a template for all your fall cocktail parties. Good luck, and gobble gobble!

Love,
Mary

PS: If you're scared to try my Turkey with Mini Pumpkin Muffins that were featured in *People* magazine (how's that for a shameless plug?), don't sweat it. Take the pressure off yourself and relish the comfort of knowing that in addition to it being a day of gratitude, it is also a day where disastrous entertaining mistakes are being made throughout the country. So roll up those sleeves and get baking.

TURKEY WITH CRANBERRY ON MINI PUMPKIN MUFFINS

1¼ cups all-purpose flour

½ cup dark brown sugar

1 teaspoon baking powder

1 teaspoon baking soda

½ teaspoon salt

½ teaspoon ground cinnamon

¼ teaspoon ground nutmeg

¾ cup canned pumpkin

⅔ cup whole milk

½ cup vegetable oil

2 eggs, beaten

4 to 6 slices leftover turkey

One 14-ounce can cranberry sauce

These muffins are a great way to use up leftover turkey or celebrate the flavors of Thanksgiving any time of year. You can also spice them up by using a jalapeño-cranberry sauce for a little kick. Another great use of leftover turkey is a turkey, Brie, and cranberry grilled cheese.

YIELD: 24 MINI MUFFINS
PREP TIME: 15 MINUTES • COOK TIME: 15 MINUTES

1. Preheat the oven to 350°F. Grease two 12-cup mini muffin pans and set aside. If you do not have two muffin pans, then please repeat twice to make 24 pieces.

2. In a bowl, mix the flour, sugar, baking powder, baking soda, salt, cinnamon, and nutmeg and set aside.

3. In a separate bowl, combine the pumpkin, milk, oil, and eggs and blend. Stir the dry ingredients into the pumpkin mixture.

4. Fill the muffin cups three-quarters full. Bake for 15 minutes.

5. Let cool for 20 minutes. Once cool, remove the muffins from the pan and slice each muffin in half horizontally.

6. Place sliced turkey and a dollop of cranberry sauce on the bottom halves and close with the muffin tops.

7. Serve on a small platter or pass as a small bite.

Party Prep Playlist

"Sing for Your Supper" (The Mamas & the Papas), "Ain't No Mountain High Enough" (Diana Ross), "Charlie Brown" Thanksgiving Theme (Vince Guaraldi), "The Thanksgiving Song" (Adam Sandler), "Thanks for the Memory" (Ella Fitzgerald), "Gratitude" (Earth, Wind & Fire), "Pleasant Valley Sunday" (The Monkees), "Thank You" (Sly and the Family Stone), "Thank You" (Led Zeppelin), "Shelter from the Storm" (Bob Dylan), "Stick with Me" (Nicki Bluhm and the Gramblers), "Harvest Moon" (Neil Young)

MASHED POTATO POPOVERS WITH MOZZARELLA

This is a variation on a recipe passed down by my Aunt Carol's Aunt Minnie. I love anything with melted cheese in it, and the first time my aunt served these at Thanksgiving, I was hooked. The bread crumbs and Parmesan give the potatoes a delcious crisp crust. A real crowd-pleaser.

YIELD: 24 POPOVERS
PREP TIME: 20 MINUTES • COOK TIME: 25 MINUTES

3 cups cooked mashed potatoes

2 teaspoons chopped fresh parsley

2 teaspoons grated Parmesan cheese

2 egg yolks, lightly beaten

1 teaspoon whole milk

1 cup shredded low-moisture mozzarella

¼ cup seasoned Italian bread crumbs

1 teaspoon each salt and pepper

Extra-virgin olive oil

1. Preheat the oven to 350°F. Grease two 12-cup mini muffin pans with olive oil.

2. In a large bowl, add the mashed potatoes, parsley, Parmesan, egg yolks, milk, ½ cup of the mozzarella (save the rest for topping), and ⅓ cup of the bread crumbs (save the rest for topping). Stir together and season with the salt and pepper.

3. With a mini (25mm) ice cream scoop, portion the mashed potato mixture into the muffin pans.

4. Top with the remaining mozzarella and bread crumbs.

5. Bake for 25 minutes, or until the tops are melted and golden brown.

6. Serve on a small decorative platter or pass as a small bite.

MINI PECAN & ROSEMARY PIES

Mini pies are a perfect party dessert, as you can pop them in your mouth without a fork.

YIELD: 24 MINI PIES
PREP TIME: 50 MINUTES • COOK TIME: 20 MINUTES

Pastry Dough

- 1½ cups all-purpose flour
- 2 tablespoons granulated sugar
- ¾ teaspoon salt
- 7 tablespoons very cold unsalted butter, cut into small pieces
- 1 egg, lightly beaten
- 2 tablespoons cold water

Filling

- ½ cup dark brown sugar
- 6 tablespoons honey
- 2 tablespoons unsalted butter, plus additional for buttering pans
- ¼ teaspoon vanilla extract
- ⅛ teaspoon salt
- 4 fresh rosemary sprigs
- ½ cup pecans
- 2 eggs

1. For the pastry dough: In a bowl, mix together the flour, sugar, and salt.

2. Using a pastry cutter, mix the cold butter into the flour mixture until it looks like wet sand.

3. Add the egg and work it into the butter mixture until just combined.

4. Use your hands to lightly press the clumps of dough into a ball. If the dough is too dry, add a tablespoon of cold water. Wrap in plastic wrap and chill the dough for at least 30 minutes.

5. For the filling: Make it while the dough rests. In a medium saucepan over low heat, combine the sugar, honey, butter, vanilla, and salt. Add the rosemary and bring to a boil. Simmer for 1 minute and turn off the heat. Let the mixture steep for at least 10 minutes. The longer it steeps, the stronger the flavor will be.

6. Preheat the oven to 350°F. Grease two 12-cup mini muffin pans with butter and refrigerate.

7. Between two pieces of parchment or wax paper, roll the dough to ¼ inch thick. Use a 2½-inch circle cutter to cut out 24 rounds. Work each round into the wells of the muffin pans. Chill for 30 minutes.

8. Toast the pecans for 10 minutes on a baking sheet. Coarsely chop about three-quarters of the nuts, leaving 24 whole.

9. Remove the rosemary from the sugar mixture and lightly beat in the eggs.

10. Add the chopped pecans and pour the filling into the prepared pans. Place 1 whole pecan on the top of each tart and bake for 20 minutes.

11. Remove the pies from the pans and let them cool on a rack.

12. Serve on a small platter or tiered stand or as part of the Mini Pie/Brownie Stand snacktivity (see page 22).

MINI PUMPKIN-CARAMEL BROWNIES

YIELD: 24 BROWNIES
PREP TIME: 15 MINUTES • COOK TIME: 30 MINUTES

1. Preheat the oven to 350°F and grease a 9 x 13-inch pan.

2. For the brownies: Melt the butter and chocolate in a double boiler, stirring occasionally. When smooth, let cool slightly.

3. In a large bowl, whisk together the eggs, sugars, vanilla, and salt. Stir in the chocolate mixture, and once it is thoroughly combined, add the flour. Set aside.

4. For the pumpkin swirl: In a medium bowl, whisk together the egg, softened cream cheese, and pumpkin.

5. In a separate bowl, combine the flour, sugar, cinnamon, and nutmeg and mix into the pumpkin mixture. Set aside.

6. For the caramel: In a medium saucepan, combine the sugar and water. Bring to medium-high heat to just before a boil and then reduce to a simmer. The mixture will begin to melt and brown around the edges. Swirl slightly to combine.

7. Once the mixture is caramel in color and liquid, at about 325°F, remove from the heat and add the heavy cream and vanilla. The mixture will boil up. Whisk together until smooth and then stir in the salt. Set aside and allow to cool.

8. Pour the brownie batter into the pan and then pour the pumpkin swirl as a layer on top.

9. Slowly drizzle horizontal lines of caramel across the top of the pumpkin batter. Space the lines about ½ inch apart to make a grid.

10. With a knife, pull the lines vertically to create a diamond pattern. Repeat every ½ inch.

11. Bake for 30 minutes. Let cool completely and then chill in the refrigerator. Cut into bite-size brownies (about 2 inches square).

12. Serve on a small platter or tiered stand by themselves or as part of the Mini Pie/Brownie Stand snacktivity (see page 22).

Brownies

- ½ pound (2 sticks) unsalted butter
- 10 ounces (10 squares) bittersweet chocolate
- 4 eggs
- 1 cup dark brown sugar
- 1 cup granulated sugar
- 2 teaspoons vanilla extract
- ½ teaspoon salt
- 1 cup all-purpose flour

Pumpkin Swirl

- 1 egg
- 8 ounces cream cheese, softened
- 1 cup canned pumpkin
- 2 tablespoons all-purpose flour
- ½ cup granulated sugar
- 1 teaspoon ground cinnamon
- ¼ teaspoon ground nutmeg

Caramel

- 1 cup granulated sugar
- ½ cup water
- ¾ cup heavy cream
- ½ teaspoon vanilla extract
- ½ teaspoon salt

TIPSY TURKEY MARTINI

What's funnier than a drunk turkey passed out on your lawn? A drunk guest passed out on your lawn. And that is exactly what you'll get if you serve this cocktail. I can't make enough of it around the holidays and no one can drink just one.

YIELD: 12 SERVINGS

- 1 32-ounce bottle of bourbon (I love Hudson bourbons)
- 1 gallon of apple cider (fresh if possible)
- 6 tablespoons agave syrup
- 2 tablespoons ground cinnamon
- 12 cinnamon sticks, as stirrers

Combine all the liquids in a drink dispenser of your choice and stir. Serve in rocks glasses garnished with a cinnamon stick.

CIDER HOUSE RULES

Beer and apple cider!? Came upon this one accidently when one of my guests wanted a shandy (beer and lemonade) and all I had in my fridge was cider. Did one of those, "Maybe this will work," and it totally did. "Good night, you princes of Maine, you kings of New England."

YIELD: 8 TO 12 SERVINGS

- 6 12-ounce bottles of your favorite beer (I love Montauk beer)
- 8 cups of apple cider (fresh if possible)
- 2 12-ounce cans ginger beer
- 4 apples, for garnish

Combine all the liquids in a drink dispenser of your choice, stir SLOWLY, and pour over ice into pilsner glasses. You can cut the apples into slices and then slice each one (see picture) and attach it to each glass as a garnish.

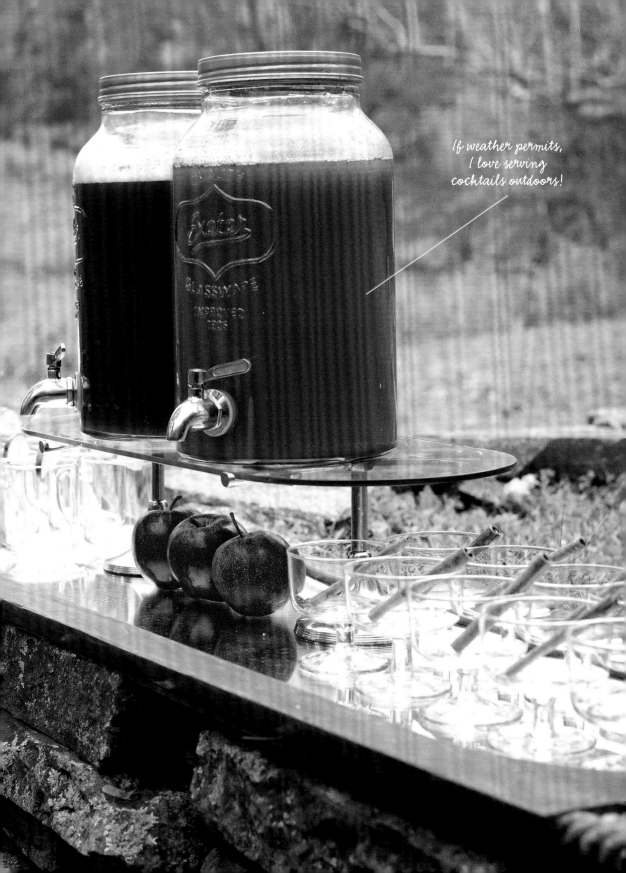

If weather permits, I love serving cocktails outdoors!

HOW TO SET A LESS IS MORE BAR

With so many options, Thanksgiving is a great holiday to set a scaled-down bar. No need to empty the entire contents of your liquor cabinet (you know all those dusty bottles I'm talking about) on this holiday. Make the selections simple:

- *One white wine, one red wine, the Tipsy Turkey and Cider House Rules (served in a drink dispenser), and sparkling or flat water (served in a pitcher). That's all you need.*

- *Set up the bar early, and in the kitchen if possible. Everyone (especially early arrivals) will be in the kitchen with you either helping or hindering your last-minute prep, so keeping the bar close by will help you stay focused. With this minimal bar setup, it can also be quickly moved into the dining or living room, as the evening progresses. I'm also a huge fan of the rolling bar cart for this reason.*

- *A bowl of garnish (fresh fruit or herbs) next to your specialty cocktail container is a nice homemade touch.*

- *Start with two bottles each of red and white, and after the first hour, assess how much is gone.*

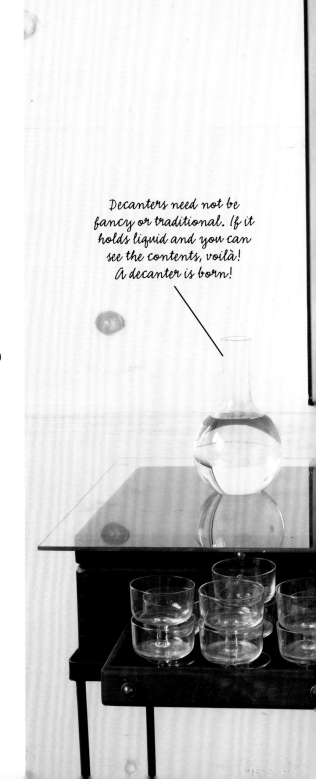

Decanters need not be fancy or traditional. If it holds liquid and you can see the contents, voilà! A decanter is born!

Lining a drawer with aluminum foil turns any piece of furniture into a ready-to-go bar.

Butternut squash, split pea, and
mushroom — store bought!

bacon

chopped
basil

chopped nuts

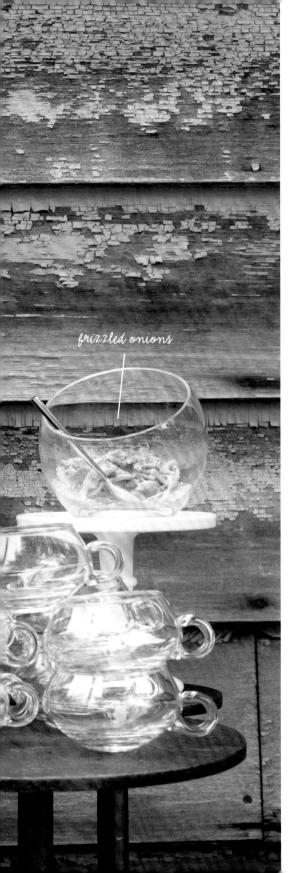

frizzled onions

SOUP SIPPING STATION

If you like making homemade soups, great! I never have time, so for me, store-bought or canned soups heated up and set out are a perfect solution.

- *I like glass pitchers (although make sure they're heat safe) so you can see what you're choosing. Little signs can be made if you don't have glass.*

- *I like choosing two or three different-colored soups to serve. Food can also be your décor. A nice variety—especially for fall—could be butternut squash, split pea, and mushroom.*

- *Bacon, frizzled onions, crème fraîche, chopped basil, and roasted nuts are delicious soup toppings, served in small (4-inch) bowls with demitasse spoons.*

- *Use small cups (IKEA has great ones) for your soup, so it is more of a tasting than a whole meal. If the cups are small, spoons can be optional (one less thing to clean up).*

You can also . . .

- *Bring back the warming plate. If you don't have one, there are a zillion retro ones sold on eBay or Etsy. Newer ones are also readily available and inexpensive to purchase.*

- *Fill pitchers with warm soup and place them on the warming tray.*

MINI PIE/BROWNIE STAND

Forget full-size desserts; it's much more fun to set up a buffet of mini pies and brownies (homemade or store-bought) with lots of toppings so that everyone gets a variety of flavors rather than filling up on one big piece.

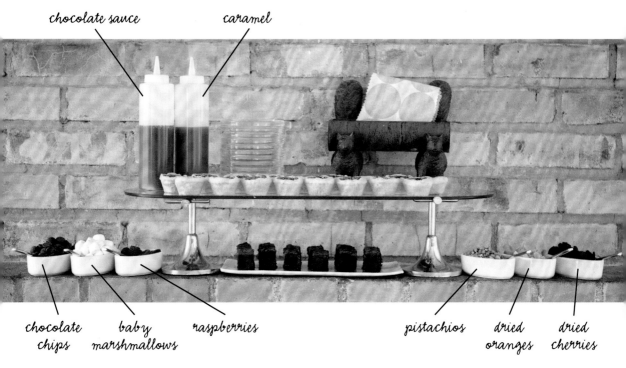

chocolate sauce   *caramel*

chocolate chips   *baby marshmallows*   *raspberries*   *pistachios*   *dried oranges*   *dried cherries*

- *Display your homemade Mini Pumpkin-Caramel Brownies and Mini Pecan & Rosemary Pies, or assorted store-bought mini pies and brownies.*

- *Using a combination of three-tiered stands and flat plates, create a dessert shop right in your dining room or any room you choose to serve dessert. I love the combination of high and low on food buffets.*

- *Fill small (4-inch) bowls with toppings such as sprinkles, nuts, and fruits. Don't forget your demi spoons for each.*

- *Fill clear squirt bottles (these can be found in stores such as Michaels and The Container Store) with caramel and chocolate sauces.*

A few more ideas (that are not shown)

- *Cover a whipped cream can with a piece of construction or crafting paper to make it match your party décor. Or make homemade whipped cream and fill a pastry bag for your guests to pipe themselves. It can get messy, but they'll have fun trying.*

- *Wanna go super cute and crafty? Then buy mini dessert boxes (these can also be found at Michaels and The Container Store), so your guests can take their pies to go.*

- *One pot of black coffee (can be made ahead and kept warm till serving) set out with espresso cups, milk, and rock candy stirrers are a great companion to the stand and give your guests a nice little spot of caffeine!*

Hangover Kit Assembly

Just in case your guests had too many Tipsy Turkeys and the food was indeed too small, a hangover kit containing aspirin, vitaminwater, and a soothing eye mask makes a perfect party favor.

CAN THE WAITERS COME DRESSED AS PILGRIMS?

Very early in my career, I received a call from a very prominent socialite (let's call her Sylvia Lewis). She was known as a grande dame of New York City entertaining. When Sylvia spoke, you listened. I was extremely lucky (at least, that is what she told me in that first phone call) that I was being given the opportunity to work with her and I had *one* chance to get it right. She asked me if I would meet her at her apartment to discuss her Thanksgiving dinner.

I quickly slammed down the phone, announced loudly and proudly to my office that Sylvia Lewis needed ME(!?), and ran out the door. Dressed in a green velvet pantsuit from Loehmann's and a pair of fake diamond studs from the Joan Rivers Collection (my mother buys me lots of gifts from QVC), I headed uptown, ready to meet the chicest lady in Manhattan.

When I arrived at Sylvia Lewis's palatial home, I was greeted first by her doorman (who gave me that "Good luck" look), then her butler, then her housekeeper, and then her assistant. They ushered me into the living room, which was like nothing I had ever seen before; it had a jaw-dropping view of Central Park and an art collection that would make Peggy Guggenheim green with envy.

(She also had a dog the size of a hamster that was barking so loudly, it distracted me from the fact that it—the dog—was wearing a diamond necklace, but that's another story.)

Sylvia was pleasant, but to the point. She was very busy (which she repeated three times over the course of our ten-minute meeting) and needed my utmost attention.

She began by asking her assistant if the china she wanted to use for this Thanksgiving dinner was in New York, Aspen, or Malibu. When her assistant responded that it was unfortunately in Malibu, a visibly upset Sylvia asked me, "Carrie"—I did not have the courage to correct her—"do you have *any idea* what it is like to have four homes and only three house managers?"

Having just bounced a check to Blockbuster video store . . . I did not.

She then began to list the rules that she insisted all her holiday caterers were to follow.

"I would like a Thanksgiving display that is both grand and abundant. I want four turkeys; one for display, three for eating. You are to shellac the prop turkey so that it shines and glistens like this." And with a French-manicured finger, she pointed to her coffee table.

"I want trays, tiers, and platters of traditional side dishes. If you are thinking of making one type of stuffing, don't. I want you to dazzle me with three different kinds. The same goes for the vegetables, starches, breads, and pies . . . I want food, food, and more food.

"And, if my husband is 'overserved' too much wine by your waiters, I will hold YOU personally responsible.

"Lastly . . . on Thanksgiving Day, the waiters must come dressed as Pilgrims."

"Pilgrims!!??" I asked, with a chuckle, but she did not look amused. She described the costumes, from the type of hats she wanted my staff to wear, down to the authentic black clog shoes that she wanted me to source from a website she had researched. She gestured to her assistant and a photo appeared and was handed to me.

When she was done, she asked, "Are my expectations clear, Carrie?"

All that was clear to me was that I thought this Lady Bird was nuts and that I was really scared of her. But I responded, "Yes, Mrs. Lewis, this will be the best Thanksgiving dinner you've ever had."

I spent the next two weeks begging our very loyal waiters to don the dreaded Pilgrim costumes (reluctantly they agreed, but we had to put a few extra pumpkin pies in their paychecks).

Thanksgiving Day arrived, and it was showtime. Curtain. Do or die.

My heart was beating as Sylvia entered the dining room to inspect the Thanksgiving display that we worked so hard to perfect. She carefully critiqued the entire table, down to each individual dinner roll, and when she was done, looked me in the eye, gave me a half-smile and said, "Mary, you will do very well here." While I was happy that she was so pleased with our work and that she called me by my correct name, I did panic a little. Here??? Were they *ever* going to let me go home!!???

So, you'd think that with this nod of approval, the rest of the evening would've been smooth sailing, right? Well, my friends . . . let's fast-forward through dinner.

It was immediately clear that Mr. Lewis needed no help from my waiters, as he had amply "overserved" himself and was so inebriated that he never made it from cocktails in the living room to dinner in the dining room. On top of that, it was one of those weird Thanksgivings, with an unseasonal snowstorm, so most of the guests canceled at the last minute, leaving Sylvia with six pies, three turkeys, eight trays of vegetables, a husband with a rocket buzz, and me, the caterer, in my fake Joan Rivers diamond earrings.

When I got home that night, my husband, Ryan, could see the horror on my face as he helped me unload the six bags of leftovers Sylvia instructed me to take with me.

Exhausted, I began to focus on how I could take back this lost holiday for my friends and family. I decided to invite my pals over for a leftover party the following night.

I started to think about all that Sylvia Lewis had to do in order to prove to the world that she was on top of it. I looked around my small apartment and suddenly, that old adage rang doubly true: LESS became MORE for me, in a major way. In that moment, I was very thankful that my apartment was the size of Sylvia's guest bathroom and our art collection was from IKEA instead of Sotheby's.

It also was at that moment that I came up with the idea of Mini Thanksgiving. This Thanksgiving I was going to do less with more. I decided to turn everything into miniature, bite-size versions of traditional Thanksgiving favorites.

I am so thankful for my experience with Sylvia Lewis, as I learned a lot from that dinner. But the most important lesson learned was, *no one* other than a *real* Pilgrim, should ever wear that horrible costume!

CHAPTER 2

Christmas

EAT

Papa Charlie's Mini Meatballs in Tomato Sauce

Carbonara Arancini (Rice Balls)

Mini Grilled Cheese with Fontina and OTTO
Black Truffle Honey

Mini Olive Oil Cakes with Cardamom Glaze,
Candied Orange, and Pistachios

Baked Italian Mini Doughnuts

DRINK

Sicilian Mistletoe

Italian Eggnog

PLAY

Mozzarella Bar

Deck Your Italian Doughnuts

RECOVER

The Art of Using Disposables

From December first to the twenty-second, my company (MGCE) caters more than fifty Christmas parties. Yes, that's a lot of mistletoe martinis! How do we do it? Well, it comes down to using as many entertaining shortcuts that we can, while still finding ways to infuse warmth and whimsy into each soiree. As an Italian American, Christmas for me is all about food, food, and more food, so the idea of serving just a few small bites and some bread and cheese could potentially send my Italian ancestors rolling over in their graves. However, I think I found a really nice way to take all the traditional large family meals down to a few delectable small bites that will still be packed with all the flavor (and calories) that one expects at a holiday party. The moral of this Christmas Cocktail Party is, Grandpa's meatball recipe does not need to get scratched, it just needs to be shrunk! *Buon Natale!*

Love,
Mary

P.S.: My Christmas Cocktail Party is Italian-inspired (and taken from our MARIO by Mary party menus), mostly because my two biggest food influences are my Sicilian grandfather, Charlie, and my friend and favorite food collaborator Mario Batali. Both of these men, whom I adore, possess endless knowledge of old-country recipes that are kept alive through the great tradition of communing with friends and family. For both of these men, food equals love.

PAPA CHARLIE'S MINI MEATBALLS IN TOMATO SAUCE

Meatballs

- 1 pound 85% lean ground beef
- 2 slices white bread, soaked in water or milk until moist but not falling apart
- 2 eggs, lightly beaten
- ½ yellow onion, finely chopped
- 2 tablespoons grated Romano or Parmesan cheese
- ½ teaspoon each salt and pepper
- ½ cup olive oil

Tomato Sauce

- ½ cup olive oil
- ½ yellow onion, chopped
- 1 garlic clove, chopped

  Pinch of red pepper flakes
- 1 28-ounce can crushed peeled tomatoes (San Marzano are best)
- 1 6-ounce can tomato paste
- 1 teaspoon each salt and pepper
- 1 teaspoon dried basil (just because it's winter and may be harder to come by. I always prefer fresh basil when available and if you can find it then I recommend about 1 cup chopped.)
- ¼ teaspoon dried oregano

Growing up, every Saturday we made Papa's sauce and meatballs. And if I have time, I still do. There is nothing better than serving a small bite that tells a story, brings up a yummy memory, or just feels like home. You can also make mini meatball subs with this recipe; just use your cookie cutter to cut small rounds out of a fresh loaf of Italian bread, or they're even better on warm garlic bread crisps.

YIELD: 24 MINI MEATBALLS
PREP TIME: 30 MINUTES • COOK TIME: 1 HOUR TO 3 HOURS

1. For the meatballs: In a large bowl, using a wooden spoon, thoroughly mix together the ground beef, soaked bread, eggs, onion, cheese, salt, and pepper. Using your hands, roll the mixture into quarter-size balls.

2. Add the olive oil to a medium sauté pan and heat over medium heat for 2 minutes.

3. Fry the meatballs until golden brown on all sides, and set aside to cool.

4. For the sauce: Add the olive oil to a large pot and heat on medium heat for 2 minutes.

5. Stir the onion, garlic, and red pepper flakes into the oil, and cook until the onions are translucent, about 8 minutes.

6. Add the crushed peeled tomatoes and tomato paste to the pot and mix well.

7. Add the salt and pepper, basil, and oregano and stir to mix.

8. Add the meatballs to the sauce and cook covered, on medium-low or low heat for at least 1 hour, or up to 3 hours.

9. Serve the meatballs in the sauce on a platter with toothpicks or on small plates with small forks.

CARBONARA ARANCINI (RICE BALLS)

YIELD: APPROXIMATELY 24 BITE-SIZE RICE BALLS
PREP TIME: 1 HOUR • COOK TIME: 15 MINUTES

1. For the rice balls: Cook the pancetta in a sauté pan on medium-low heat, slowly rendering it until crispy, about 8 minutes. Drain on a plate lined with paper towels.

2. In a medium bowl, combine the rice, pancetta, and remaining ingredients and mix well. Refrigerate the mixture for at least 1 hour so that it has a firm consistency.

3. Line a baking sheet with parchment paper. Using a mini (25mm) ice cream scoop or a rounded teaspoon, place individual scoops of the rice mixture onto the prepared baking sheet. Roll each scoop into an even, tight ball, using your hands.

4. For the coating: In a shallow bowl (a pie pan works well for this), add the flour and season with salt and pepper. In a second bowl, whisk the eggs. In a third bowl, add the bread crumbs. (This is the standard breading formula for most breaded and fried foods.)

5. Roll the rice balls first in the seasoned flour, then gently shake them to remove any excess flour. Next, dunk the rice balls into the egg mixture to coat them. Finally, roll the rice balls in the bread crumbs, making sure each ball is thoroughly covered. You can repeat the egg wash and bread crumb steps for an even crunchier coating. The prepared rice balls can be refrigerated for up to 1 day.

6. For frying: In a large frying pan, heat the oil for 5 minutes on medium heat. To test if the oil is hot enough to begin frying, throw a sprinkle of bread crumbs into the oil; if they bubble and sizzle right away, your oil is hot enough. Now fry one arancino first to get the timing down. *Do not* throw all your balls in at once, as they will be crowded and cause the oil temperature to drop.

7. Carefully cook the balls in the oil until all sides are golden brown, about 3 minutes. Drain on a paper towel.

8. Sprinkle with fresh-grated Romano and serve on a decorative platter or pass as a small bite.

Rice Balls

- 2 cups cooked white rice, prepared with a pinch of salt
- 6 ounces pancetta, diced fine
- 24 ounces fresh ricotta cheese
- 3 cups shredded mozzarella cheese
- 1 cup finely grated Romano cheese, plus additional for serving
- 2 eggs
- 2 tablespoons chopped fresh flat-leaf parsley
- 1 tablespoon salt
- 1 tablespoon freshly ground black pepper

Coating

- 1 cup all-purpose flour
- Salt and freshly ground black pepper
- 4 eggs
- 2 cups seasoned Italian bread crumbs

Frying

1 cup vegetable oil

MINI GRILLED CHEESE WITH FONTINA AND OTTO BLACK TRUFFLE HONEY

3 tablespoons mayonnaise

1 tablespoon Dijon-style mustard

1 tablespoon grated horseradish, drained

Salt and pepper

6 slices good white sandwich bread (I love *pain de mie*)

¼ pound fontina cheese, sliced approximately ⅛ inch thick

2 tablespoons unsalted butter, melted

OTTO Black Truffle Honey (See Resources, page 209)

Our mini grilled cheese is hands down our most popular hors d'oeuvre. Last year, I was playing in my kitchen and drizzled Mario Batali's OTTO Black Truffle Honey onto one little sandwich, and voilà, *I had created one of the greatest culinary pairings in the history of the world, like a wonderful Johnny Cash and June Carter duet. Taste these and tell me if you don't hear music!*

YIELD: 24 MINI SANDWICHES
PREP TIME: 5 MINUTES • COOK TIME: 8 TO 12 MINUTES

1. In a small bowl, stir together the mayonnaise, mustard, and horseradish. Season with salt and pepper.

2. Spread out 3 slices of the bread on a board and thinly smear with the mayonnaise-mustard mixture.

3. Top each of the 3 bread slices with 3 slices of cheese, then add a pinch of salt and pepper. Close with the remaining 3 slices of bread.

4. Brush the top pieces of bread lightly with the melted butter and place buttered side down in a nonstick sauté pan over low heat. While the buttered side is slowly browning, lightly brush the top portion of the bread with butter.

5. Once the underside is golden brown, carefully flip over to cook and brown the other side. Remove from the pan and cut each sandwich diagonally from corner to corner, creating 4 triangles, then cut each triangle in half to give you 8 mini triangles per sandwich.

6. Place on a serving tray and drizzle with the OTTO Black Truffle Honey. Serve immediately or pass as a small bite.

MINI OLIVE OIL CAKES WITH CARDAMOM GLAZE, CANDIED ORANGE, AND PISTACHIOS

YIELD: 24 BITE-SIZE CAKES

PREP TIME: 50 MINUTES • COOK TIME: 35 TO 40 MINUTES

Glaze

- 1 cup water
- ½ cup granulated sugar
- 6 tablespoons honey
- 1 tablespoons green cardamom pods, crushed
- 1 small orange

Cakes

- 3 eggs
- 1 cup granulated sugar
- 1½ cups whole milk
- 1 cup good-quality extra-virgin olive oil, plus additional for coating the pan
- 1 tablespoon candied orange zest, plus more for decorating
- 1½ cups all-purpose flour, plus additional for dusting the pan
- ½ cup coarse-ground cornmeal
- ½ teaspoon baking powder
- ½ teaspoon baking soda
- ½ teaspoon salt
- ½ cup unsalted pistachios, chopped

1. For the glaze: Bring the water, sugar, honey, and cardamom to a boil in a medium heavy saucepan, stirring until the mixture dissolves.

2. With a vegetable peeler, remove the zest from the orange in long ½-inch-wide strips. Finely julienne the strips.

3. Add the orange zest to the syrup. Reduce the heat to medium-low; simmer until the syrup is reduced to 1 cup, approximately 40 minutes.

4. Remove the zest and reserve. Strain the syrup and reserve.

5. Preheat the oven to 350°F and arrange a rack in the middle. Coat a 9 x 13-inch pan with olive oil and flour and tap out the excess.

6. For the cakes: In a large bowl, whisk together the eggs and granulated sugar until well blended and light in color. Add the milk, olive oil, and orange zest.

7. In another bowl, stir together the flour, cornmeal, baking powder, baking soda, and salt. Add the dry ingredients to the egg mixture, stirring until just blended. Do not overmix.

8. Pour the batter into the pan and smooth to make an even layer. Bake 35 to 40 minutes, until a toothpick inserted into the center comes out clean. Remove from the oven and place on a wire rack. Pierce the cake all over with a toothpick. Brush the top of the cake with some of the reserved syrup. Once absorbed, add an additional layer of syrup.

9. In a small frying pan, toast the pistachios until slightly browned. Set aside.

10. Let the cake cool in the pan. When cool, use a 1½-inch circle cookie cutter to cut out individual cakes. Top each mini cake with strips of candied orange zest and sprinkle with pistachios. Dot the top of each cake with additional syrup to set the topping.

BAKED ITALIAN MINI DOUGHNUTS

½ cup plus 2 tablespoons unsalted butter, softened

1 cup granulated sugar

2 eggs

1 cup milk

2 teaspoons vanilla extract

3 cups all-purpose flour

2 teaspoons baking powder

Pinch of salt

Later on in the chapter, you'll find a snacktivity called Deck Your Italian Doughnuts. If you want to go the extra mile and make your donuts from scratch, here's the perfect recipe. No judgment if you go for the store-bought ones instead.

YIELD: 24 MINI DOUGHNUTS

PREP TIME: 15 MINUTES • COOK TIME: 20 MINUTES

1. Preheat the oven to 325°F. Lightly oil a mini doughnut pan with cooking spray. (You can also use mini muffin pans.)

2. In a medium bowl, cream together the butter and sugar until light and fluffy. Beat in the eggs, milk, and vanilla until combined.

3. In a separate bowl, combine the flour, baking powder, and salt. Mix the flour mixture into the butter mixture until combined. Do not overmix.

4. Transfer the batter to a piping bag with a large round tip and fill each doughnut well halfway.

5. Bake for 20 minutes. Test for doneness (they should be crisp on the outside, moist on the inside). Transfer to a cooling rack or serve immediately to your guests to decorate.

Party Prep Playlist

Starting with my Papa Charlie's favorite: "Christmas Song" (Alvin and the Chipmunks), "All I Want for Christmas Is You" (Mariah Carey), "Wonderful Christmas Time" (Paul McCartney and Wings, "Dominick the Donkey" (Lou Monte), "Santa Baby" (Eartha Kitt), "Do They Know It's Christmas?" (Band Aid), "The Chanukah Song" (Adam Sandler), "Riu Chiu" (The Monkees), "That's Amore" (Dean Martin), "Lazy Mary" (Louis Prima or Lou Monte), "Because You're Mine" (Mario Lanza), "Please Come Home for Christmas" (Grace Potter & the Nocturnals), "Christmas" (Darlene Love)

SICILIAN MISTLETOE

I'm Sicilian, which makes me both fiery and romantic. This cocktail is a perfect expression of those two qualities. It also works really well drizzled over a bowl of vanilla ice cream.

YIELD: 10 TO 12 SERVINGS

2 liter bottles vodka

1 liter bottle Averna

2 cups cinnamon syrup

Maraschino cherries

Combine the vodka, Averna, and syrup, and shake to mix in a drink dispenser of your choice. Serve in martini glasses, garnished with a cherry.

ITALIAN EGGNOG

The perfect accompaniment to Deck Your Italian Doughnuts!

YIELD: 10 TO 12 SERVINGS

10 egg yolks

2¼ cups granulated sugar

1 750ml bottle white Italian sweet wine

1½ cups rum

½ gallon whole milk

2 tablespoons grated nutmeg

1. Beat the egg yolks until light in color. Add the sugar, Italian sweet wine, and rum. Stir until the sugar is dissolved. Add the milk, stirring slowly. Sprinkle the nutmeg on top.

2. Refrigerate until ready to serve. Serve in a punch bowl with either coffee mugs or punch bowl mugs and ice.

MOZZARELLA BAR

Reinvent the cheese board by purchasing three types of Italian cheeses. I like burrata, mozzarella (salted or unsalted), and ricotta because of their different textures.

- *Slice the cheese before serving to make it easier for your guests to help themselves.*

- *Make that cheese the star. Set the main attraction above the rest of the items to show that's what you should take first and everything else is the chorus.*

- *Don't forget cheese knives and forks and spoons for each bowl or topping.*

- *Items like eggplant caponata, roasted peppers, roasted tomatoes, romesco sauce, and olive tapenades are wonderful complements for cheeses, and all can be store-bought if you don't have the time to make them.*

- *Three meats that are easy to find and go great with these cheeses are prosciutto (thinly sliced), pepperoni, and Italian dried sausage. Set them on a wooden cheese board below the cheese.*

- *Balsamic vinegar and olive oil are a must at this station. Pre-slice bread (but not all of it) just before your guests arrive to preserve freshness. Display the remaining bread for decoration and freeze the loaves you do not use for your next party.*

- *Small (4-inch) plates and forks are all you need for this station; just don't forget the cocktail napkins.*

- *Use classic holiday movies as your décor. A Charlie Brown Christmas or It's A Wonderful Life playing on the TV and a few twinkly candles on your table can be all the décor (and lighting) you need to make your party feel festive.*

DECK YOUR ITALIAN DOUGHNUTS

Dessert-only parties are *totally* acceptable at this time of the year. The real official Italian doughnut is the *zeppole.* However, frying and timing can be hard to pull off at home, and why mess with something that only the San Gennaro festival can pull off perfectly? A bar with Baked Italian Mini Doughnuts (page 38) will work better and they can sit out longer.

- *Everyone thinks that baked items need to be transferred from the baking tray to a plate. Save that step and serve straight from the oven on the tray . . . this gives it a very homemade feel (even if you are just warming up store-bought items). Set some nice napkins or tea towels under the tray.*

- *Pick some good "glues." Icing and chocolate and caramel sauce are great to smear on top of the doughnuts so that all the delicious toppings will stick.*

- *You can also fill mini squeeze bottles with caramel or chocolate sauce to inject into the doughnuts.*

- *Place your unique toppings—bacon, sprinkles, powdered sugar, dried or fresh fruit—in small bowls, to give your guests the opportunity to deck their doughnuts properly.*

- *It's absolutely fine to use store-bought doughnuts. You'll need all the extra time you can get during the holiday season, and this is a great time-saver.*

NOW FOR THE EGGNOG . . . AND SOME GENERAL HOLIDAY DRINKING TIPS

- *Don't be a holiday drunk—drink consistently all year and embarrass yourself at all times. This way, your bad holiday behavior won't stand out and, instead, will be anticipated. This is not the party to skimp on the nonalcoholic beverages, either, since most people are perpetually hungover during this time of year.*

- *The punch bowl or drink dispenser is your best friend during the holidays. Use any of the recipes I've provided in this chapter, dump the ingredients in the bowl/dispenser, and enjoy your party. Guests can help themselves and you're not playing bartender all night.*

- *Want to know how to save that opened champagne for New Year's? Put a spoon in the top of your bottle of sparkly and place it in the fridge. This will conserve the bubbles for a few days.*

- *Come to think of it, do you want to avoid going back to the liquor store at all between Christmas and the new year? Make sure you buy sufficient drinks for both holidays at one time. Remember the simple math:*

- *6 glasses of wine per bottle, 7 glasses of champagne per bottle; 12 to14 drinks per spirits bottle.*

- *AND estimate 2 drinks per guest per party. Too much math? Tell your guests to BYOB. Totally okay this time of year!*

Some Extra Play Ideas

Holiday lights aren't just for the tree. Fill clear vases with strings of holiday lights (now there are battery-operated ones) to give your room a little extra sparkle.

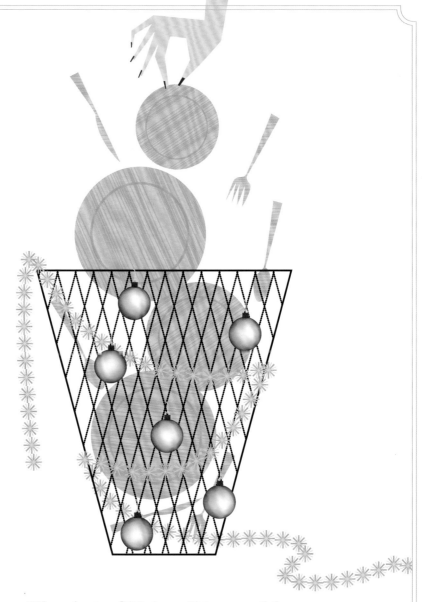

The Art of Using Disposables

Holiday time is the perfect time for using disposable plates. There are so many great eco-friendly disposable plates and flatware available that both look great and will save you cleanup time the next day.

JUST IN CASE SANTA IS ITALIAN

It was the night before Christmas and I was eight years old. My sister, Nanette, and I had worked hard to organize the perfect plate of cookies, glass of milk, and note to leave for Santa. Once it was all arranged by the fireplace, as my mother recalls it, I was distinctly dissatisfied with our offering. According to her, I went back into the kitchen, took out some prosciutto, and started rolling it around some breadsticks. When my mom asked what I was doing, I looked up and said, "Just in case Santa is Italian."

For some, tinsel and colorful lights may conjure up childhood memories of Christmas, but for me, it's *cardone* and *cucidati.*

I have one man to thank for this, my grandfather Papa Charlie—my hero, and one of the funniest men I've ever known. A Sicilian American with a heart of gold, who treasured his family above all—with food, drink, and a pack of Kent cigarettes a close second.

In my family, *cooking,* not *shopping,* kicked off our holiday season, with Papa Charlie at the helm of our Sicilian-American ship. His job was to keep us all on schedule for the Main Event—Christmas Eve dinner.

Two weeks prior, we made Sicilian Christmas cookies called *cucidati.* Papa told us it was a recipe passed down by Italian nuns from the town in Sicily from which we hail, Polizzi Generosa. While I'm not sure if his story was true, the way he told it (always with a dirty joke about a nun) made me laugh every time. He would take out his old metal meat grinder for its yearly duty and instead of meats, he would load in raisins, piñoli nuts, dates, and molasses. He would let me turn the handle, always followed by him pretending that I caught his finger in the grinder. This, of course, would require him to take a "medicinal" swig of wine before continuing with the baking process. To be honest, I never liked the taste of these cookies, but I couldn't resist the part when his finger would get stuck.

The week before Christmas was for shopping and for making the bolognese. I felt so special because he chose to take my sister and me on this annual trip—a ritual, really—heading into Brooklyn in his gray Cadillac. First we would stop at the butcher for the ground meat (veal and pork), then the cheese shop for the wheel of Parmesan, then the ravioli store, and finally to the supermarket to get the mushrooms, *cardones,* and artichokes. Of course, all the store owners knew my grandfather by name and they always gave my sister and me some special treats. Once, a butcher gave us gold crosses that he kept in his pocket as if they were pieces of candy.

Finally, on the morning of Christmas Eve, our kitchen would be set up like a prepping station at a busy restaurant. My sister and I would stuff the artichokes and mushrooms, while Papa would fry the *cardones,* a cigarette dangling out of the side of his mouth the entire time.

And then it was the Feast of the Seven Fishes. But don't look to me for a recipe. Papa and I shared a common hatred for the smell of fried fish, so he made me what he called "Mariuccia's Pasta," aka carbonara, MY FAVORITE and the reason

I've included it here as a small bite. While my family would feast on eel and *baccalà*, Papa and I would have a delicious plate of pasta with just the perfect amount of pecorino Romano, bacon (pancetta was too fancy for us), egg, and black pepper, like we were our own special supper club.

I'm now older, Papa is gone, and I realize that those memories, smells, and tastes were more precious than any of the wrapped gifts I received as a child. These memories are sacred to me. Here were three generations of people together in a room, sharing their recipes, stories, secrets, all the while laughing, crying (remembering the recipes of loved ones who had passed), and singing, always singing. I consider myself lucky that an artichoke can make me smile and remind me of Papa's laugh; and that a cookie recipe, which may or may not have been created by nuns, allows me to recall the smell of my grandfather's smoke-filled Cadillac. I keep these memories alive by allowing the food that I serve at my Christmas parties to tell Papa's story over and over again. I keep that tradition and, of course, I still leave out some prosciutto-wrapped bread sticks every Christmas Eve . . . just in case Santa is Italian.

to: Santa
love, Mary

CHAPTER 3

New Year's Eve

EAT

Mini Sausage and Egg Grilled Cheese

Mini Kale and Fontina Breakfast Pies

Banana Pancake Bites

Mini Chocolate Chip and
Candied Bacon Pancakes

DRINK

Champagne Jell-O Shots

Blueberry Breakfast Cocktail

PLAY

Hash Bash

Frittata, Your Way

Bloody Mary Bar

RECOVER

The Morning After Refrigerator Preparedness

A midnight breakfast Cocktail Party!? Really!?

As I mentioned in the previous chapter, Christmas is one of the busiest times of the year for my business, so when clients start to inquire what to do for their New Year's Eve parties, I almost always recommend pajamas, champagne, and episodes of *The Honeymooners* . . . in bed! But one year, a very special client did get me out of bed to plan her New Year's Eve disco party. She wanted the disco element to be a surprise, so the dinner portion of the evening took place in her house, but secretly we had turned their garage into a late-night disco. At midnight, she led her guests into the garage for the big reveal. I have to say, it was one of my favorite party moments; her guests were completely surprised and really thrilled to dance themselves into the New Year. Since it was late, we created a menu made up of mini versions of everyone's favorite breakfast foods and one big bagel buffet with lots of spreads.

Perhaps turning your garage into a disco is a bit extreme, but serving breakfast for an evening party is totally acceptable on New Year's Eve or any holiday that you think will go past midnight or into the next day. Not a late-night person? These recipes and tips work for a celebratory brunch, baby shower, or daytime event.

This is a great way to shake things up, and trust me—a mini sausage and egg grilled cheese sandwich works no matter what time of day you serve it!

Love,
Mary

MINI SAUSAGE AND EGG GRILLED CHEESE

5 eggs

¼ cup whole milk

3 tablespoons unsalted butter, divided

Salt and pepper

8 ounces breakfast sausage, removed from casing or finely chopped

1 cup shredded cheese blend (preferably pepper Jack and Cheddar)

6 slices regular white or whole wheat bread

Ketchup

I love sausage with my eggs, but this recipe also works great with bacon, ham, or avocado.

YIELD: 24 MINI TRIANGLES
PREP TIME: 15 MINUTES • COOK TIME: 18 TO 24 MINUTES

1. In a bowl, whisk together the eggs with the milk and set aside.

2. In a nonstick sauté pan, melt 1 tablespoon of the butter on medium-low heat. Add the egg mixture, a pinch each of salt and pepper, and stir until scrambled. Remove the eggs from the pan and let cool slightly.

3. In the same pan, add the sausage and cook, stirring until it is cooked through and lightly golden brown. Spoon the sausage into the egg mixture and fold in to combine. Allow the mixture to cool. Add the shredded cheeses and combine thoroughly. Adjust the seasonings to taste.

4. In the microwave or in a separate pan, melt remaining 2 tablespoons butter for brushing on the sandwiches.

5. On a clean work surface, spread out 3 slices of bread and fill each slice with a thin layer of the egg mixture. Close with the remaining 3 slices of bread and brush the top of each sandwich with the melted butter.

6. Preheat a nonstick pan on low heat. Add the sandwiches buttered-side down, one at a time, and cook for approximately 2 minutes or until golden brown. While the bottom is cooking, brush the tops of the sandwiches with melted butter.

7. Carefully flip the sandwiches over and brown the other sides. Set on a cutting board and cut slices diagonally from corner to corner, creating 4 triangles, then cut each triangle in half to give you 8 mini triangles per sandwich.

8. Serve each piece with a dot of ketchup.

MINI KALE AND FONTINA BREAKFAST PIES

YIELD: 24 PIES
PREP TIME: 40 MINUTES • COOK TIME: 20 MINUTES

1. Preheat the oven to 400°F. Line baking sheets with parchment paper and set aside.

2. For the Dough: In a food processor, combine the flour, baking powder, sugar, and salt. Add the cold butter and pulse until the butter resembles pea-size pieces. Don't overmix. Drizzle in the cold water. The dough should form a solid mass. Add 1 or 2 additional tablespoons of water if needed for the dough to stick together. Remove the dough from the processor and refrigerate for at least 20 minutes.

3. Place the dough on a lightly floured surface. Flour a rolling pin and roll the dough out to ¼ inch thick. Cut out circles of the dough using a 3-inch cookie cutter. Place the circles onto the paper-lined baking sheets and set in the refrigerator until ready to use.

4. For the Filling: In a bowl, whisk together the eggs with ¼ cup of the milk and set aside.

5. In a nonstick sauté pan, melt 2 tablespoons of the butter on medium-low heat. Add the shallots and cook for 2 minutes, stirring occasionally, then add the kale and cook until wilted. Season to taste with salt and pepper. Add the egg and milk mixture and stir to create scrambled eggs. Remove and set aside in a bowl to cool slightly.

6. Using the same pan, add the remaining 2 tablespoons butter over medium heat. Stir in the flour to make a roux, stirring constantly for 4 minutes. Whisk in the remaining 1¼ cups milk slowly to avoid any lumps. Keep stirring and simmer for 5 minutes, until the mixture thickens slightly. Remove from heat and stir in the fontina. Season with salt and pepper.

7. Pour the cheese mixture into the kale and egg mixture, stir, and let cool slightly. It should look like creamy scrambled eggs.

8. Top each dough round with 1 to 2 teaspoons of filling, then a second round, sealing the edges with a fork. Brush the top of each pie generously with the beaten egg.

9. Bake the pies for 15 to 20 minutes, or until the tops are flaky and golden. Cool slightly before serving.

Dough

- 1 cup all-purpose flour, plus additional for the rolling pin and work surface
- 2 teaspoons baking powder
- ½ teaspoon granulated sugar
- ½ teaspoon salt
- ¼ cup (½ stick) unsalted butter, cut into cubes and chilled
- ⅓ cup cold water
- 1 egg, lightly beaten

Filling

- 4 eggs
- 1½ cups milk
- 4 tablespoons unsalted butter, divided
- 2 shallots, peeled and diced
- 1 bunch kale, cleaned, spun dried, destemmed, and chopped (can pulse in food processor if preferred)
- Salt and black pepper
- 2 tablespoons all-purpose flour
- 1 cup shredded fontina cheese

BANANA PANCAKE BITES

If making cute little pancakes is a bit too precious for you, this batter can also be poured into two greased mini muffin tins to make 24 Banana Pancake Muffins.

3 medium bananas

2 cups all-purpose flour

½ cup granulated sugar

4 teaspoons baking powder

½ teaspoon baking soda

½ teaspoon salt

2 cups buttermilk

2 eggs

3 teaspoons vanilla extract

2 tablespoons melted butter

1½ cups mini chocolate chips

Maple syrup (optional)

YIELD: 24 BITE-SIZE PANCAKES
PREP TIME: 20 MINUTES • COOK TIME: 18 TO 24 MINUTES

1. Peel both bananas. Mash one with a fork and cut the other into very thin slices for garnish.

2. In a medium bowl, sift together the flour, sugar, baking powder, baking soda, and salt and set aside.

3. In a separate bowl, whisk together the buttermilk, egg, mashed banana, vanilla, and melted butter.

4. Pour the liquid ingredients into the dry ingredients and mix to combine, taking care not to overmix.

5. Pour the batter into a squeeze bottle to make the pancakes consistent in size and store in the refrigerator for at least 20 minutes.

6. Coat a medium nonstick skillet with nonstick spray or a little butter. Turn the heat on to medium-low (not too hot).

7. When the pan is ready, gently squeeze out the batter into quarter-size pancakes; dot with the mini chocolate chips. Allow to cook about 2 minutes, then gently flip for an additional 2 minutes or until golden in color on both sides.

8. Place the pancakes on a plate with a paper towel over them to avoid drying out.

9. When ready to serve, gently warm the pancake bites in a 325°F oven for a few minutes. To serve, stack 3 pancakes with a banana slice on top and pierce through the center with a small clear skewer or fancy toothpick. For extra-fancy pancake bites, drizzle with maple syrup.

MINI CHOCOLATE CHIP AND CANDIED BACON PANCAKES

3 thick-cut bacon slices

1 tablespoon dark brown sugar

¼ teaspoon ground cinnamon

2 cups all-purpose flour

2 tablespoons granulated sugar

½ teaspoon salt

1 teaspoon baking powder

½ teaspoon baking soda

1 cup buttermilk

¾ cup milk

2 eggs, separated

4 tablespoons (½ stick) unsalted butter, melted

2 ounces mini semisweet chocolate chips

Vegetable oil

Maple syrup (optional)

All of my favorite sweet and salty breakfast flavors in one satisfying bite.

YIELD: 24 BITE-SIZE PANCAKES
PREP TIME: 30 MINUTES • COOK TIME: 18 TO 24 MINUTES

1. Preheat the oven to 350°F and line a baking sheet with foil. Set a wire rack on top and coat it with nonstick spray.

2. Lay the bacon in strips on the rack and sprinkle with the brown sugar and cinnamon. Bake for 20 to 25 minutes, until the bacon is crisp and caramelized. Remove from the oven and allow to cool. Once the bacon is cool enough to handle, chop it into fine pieces.

3. Lower the oven temperature to 200°F.

4. In a mixing bowl, combine the flour, granulated sugar, salt, baking powder, and baking soda.

5. In another bowl, whisk together the buttermilk, milk, egg yolks, and melted butter. Slowly add the dry ingredients to the wet ingredients until just combined. Stir in the chocolate chips and candied bacon, reserving some bacon for garnish.

6. Beat the egg whites in another bowl until stiff peaks form. Fold one-third of the egg whites at a time into the batter until well incorporated.

7. Heat a griddle pan over medium-high heat and lightly coat with vegetable oil or cooking spray. Ladle the batter, 1 tablespoon at a time, onto the hot griddle and cook until small bubbles appear on the top. Flip and cook until the other side is golden brown. Continue with the remaining batter and keep the finished pancakes warm in the oven.

8. To serve, pierce 3 pancakes through the center with a small clear skewer or fancy toothpick to look like a little stack. Top each with a piece of crispy bacon.

9. Drizzle with maple syrup before serving (optional).

CHAMPAGNE JELL-O SHOTS

YIELD: 12 SHOTS

1 3-ounce package white peach Jell-O

2 cups boiling water

1 cup cold champagne

Decorative sugars for dipping (in the baking section of most supermarkets)

1. Dissolve the Jell-O in the boiling water, add the cold champagne, and stir to combine.

2. Pour into ice cube trays and put in fridge to set.

3. Pour pastel sugars onto individual small plates.

4. Once the Jell-O squares are set, remove from the trays, and dip the tops of each square cube into the pastel-colored sugars.

5. Chill in the fridge for 30 minutes to 1 hour until time to serve. Jell-O can be made the night before or morning of your party.

BLUEBERRY BREAKFAST COCKTAIL

YIELD: 12 SERVINGS

1 1/3 liters raspberry-flavored vodka

12 ounces fresh lemon juice

12 ounces Triple Sec

2 handfuls of blueberries, half for the cocktail, half for garnish

1. Pour the vodka, lemon juice, Triple Sec, and half of the fresh blueberries into a drink dispenser of your choice and mix well.

2. Serve in champagne glasses over ice with additional blueberries in the bottom of each glass.

ADDITIONAL NEW YEAR'S EVE TIPS

EAT

Midnight breakfast is fine, but I still think New Year's deserves an elevated culinary moment. How about serving caviar and bagels? Set out assorted bagels, spreads, and caviar. A small tin of caviar can be displayed in a bowl of chilled ice, which will keep it at a proper temperature. It's a great dressed-up yet dressed-down statement.

DRINK

It doesn't have to be champagne just because it's New Year's Eve. I have so many clients who don't like champagne, but feel obligated to serve it. It's your house, so serve what you like. Even if it's a case of PBR. Just be sure to pour it into a champagne flute or coupe to make it festive.

PLAY

I'm a huge fan of an impromptu dance party for two or two hundred after the ball drops. Make sure your iPod is fully loaded with high-energy celebration songs and have a dance party. Summon Dick Clark's spirit by turning your living room into American Bandstand. It's totally okay to dance in pajamas and socks.

hot sauce   sausage   sour cream   Cheddar cheese

HASH BASH

Everyone *loves* mason jars. Who needs plates (especially for this station) when you can load them up, place the lid on, and shake? Hmmm . . . that actually gives me an idea for a Shake and Bake Party (next book?).

- *Always set your snacktivity station in the order you want your guests to assemble their meals. Start with the jars, then the hash browns, then the toppings, then the lid, then the fork and napkin at the end. Forks and napkins can also go in the mason jar for service.*

- *Set your toppings out in advance: caramelized onions, diced peppers, bacon, sausage, Cheddar cheese, sour cream, and hot sauce. All of these items can be prepped* *in advance of the party and served at room temperature.*

- *Heat the hash browns (store-bought or homemade) in a skillet and serve on a warming tray (I told you I love warming trays) or in front of a fire (as shown), so your guests can fill their jars with the hash browns and then toppings of their choice then seal the jar and shake. This mason jar shake method works great with salads as well.*

FRITTATA, YOUR WAY

Don't get scared by the fancy Italian name for an omelet. A frittata is a very easy thing to make that can be cooked in advance of your guests arriving and then just reheated and served. Find your favorite frittata recipe (I love spinach and provolone frittata) and cook it in a 10-inch nonstick frying pan (to serve 8 to 10 guests).

crushed red pepper flakes

proscuitto

banana pancake bites

spinach & provolone frittata

ricotta

mini kale and fontina breakfast pies

- Set toppings out in advance: ricotta, Parmesan cheese, prosciutto, and red pepper flakes.

- Five minutes before it's time to serve, just reheat the frittata and place on your already set frittata bar.

- Pre-slice so that portions are easier to take and will guarantee you have control over the number of guests you've prepared for.

- A 4-inch plate, fork, and napkin is all your guests will need to enjoy this snacktivity.

BLOODY MARY BAR

This bar can be served on New Year's Eve night or the morning after.

scallions & bacon

Bloody Mary mix

carrots lemons radishes olives horseradish

- *Premake your favorite Bloody Mary recipe and fill a drink dispenser.*

- *Place out unique toppings: bacon, celery, scallions, horseradish, radishes, carrots, lemons, olives, salt, and pepper.*

- *Set out highball glasses and small 4-inch plates in case your guests want some extra toppings with their Bloody Marys.*

- *You can also pre-cut and serve scallions or celery and bacon in glasses so they are all set for the big pour.*

The Morning After Refrigerator Preparedness

Plan ahead so that the next day is all about resting and recharging.
Make sure the fridge is stocked with eggs, cheese, & bacon (or any
hangover remedy you desire), so you don't have to leave the house.
Those of us who live in cities with diners that deliver can be a bit more
lazy, but those of us with limited delivery options should prep well!

THE ONE NIGHT I WAS COOL

My sister, Nanette, was (is) HOT! In my head, when I look back at our childhood and recall time spent with my older sister, she always appears to be moving in slow motion, with a wind machine blowing her hair back, smoke rolling in from the sides of the camera, caressing her every movement. She had every conceivably perfect '80s fashion accessory, from her aerobicized Jane Fonda butt encased in a metallic lavender thong leotard down to her E.G. Smith legwarmers and shiny black hair that fell perfectly to her size 0 waist. She was as tan as the Girl from Ipanema, 365 days a year. She drove a chic European convertible, had lots of friends, and wore head-to-toe white leather as she danced to Chaka Khan.

Suffice to say, she rarely spoke to me . . .

We had no similar interests, particularly when it came to food. She liked vanilla. I liked chocolate. She survived on fat-free bran muffins, while I ate pizza and calzones (often at the same time). After school on Fridays, she could be found hanging out at the oh-so-cool frozen yogurt shop, and I could be found with my friend Kappy at Bennigan's for our standing pig-out, where we would double down on potato skins and mozzarella sticks. While my sister was up on hot/cool tunes, I listened to The Monkees (not so cool for a kid growing up in 1986), and while she spent the entire summer working at a hot summer day camp, getting water splashed on her on purpose by even-hotter lifeguards, I spent an entire summer in my bedroom trying to "save the Princess" in *Super Mario Brothers*.

So, what does any of this stroll down Sisterly Lane have to do with New Year's Eve, or, more importantly, your party!?

Well, one year I was feeling particularly uncool, realizing that I would be spending yet another New Year's at home with my parents and their friends singing doo-wop in our basement. Nanette, of course, had amazing New Year's Eve plans that involved a trip into Manhattan to the opening of what was sounding like *the* hot new nightclub. On her way out, she and her gorgeous boyfriend stopped by my room. I remember her white leather headband held her perfectly primped Paul Mitchell hair in place, and she asked what I was doing that night. Sort of rare, because she didn't usually bother talking to me. I told her that I was thinking about watching a double feature of *A Hard Day's Night* and *Help*. Very uncool.

At 11:45, just as the smell of my sister's boyfriend's Drakkar Noir cologne had dissipated from my bedroom, the unthinkable happened.

My beautiful perfect supercool '80s sister walked into my room (precisely at the part where George was singing "Norwegian Wood"). I was startled by her early return home from NYC, so much so that I was convinced there clearly had been a tragic accident, culminating in the double deaths of both Boy George and Simon Le Bon.

She sat down next to me, tugged off her leather, and said, "I can't let my little sister spend New Year's with the Beatles alone in her bedroom." Halfway to the city, I guess she felt some love in her heart for me, turned around, and headed home, bailing on her friends.

And if the shock of her return didn't kill me, what happened next almost did. She asked *me* what I wanted to do with the rest of *our* night! Without skipping a beat, we headed toward the kitchen and got to work. We looked through the cabinets and, after a bit of deliberation and some negotiation, we made chocolate chip pancakes and scrambled eggs with bacon. There we were, mixing, frying, and laughing with Dick Clark on the tube and doo-wop playing in the basement. It was one of the best nights I can remember from that time. Just shortly after midnight, she even let me dance a little to Chaka Khan with her in the living room. And on that night . . . I was cool.

WORK HARD & BE NICE TO PEOPLE

CHAPTER 4

Game Day

EAT
Mini Buffalo Chicken Grilled Cheese

MACO (Mac and Cheese Taco) with Guacamole

Banoffee Cream Pie in a Mug

"Chopretzato" (Chocolate, Pretzel, Potato Chip
Pudding in a Mug)

DRINK
Beerbon

Beergarita

PLAY
Dress Your Pigs in a Blanket

DIY Grilled Cheese Bar

RECOVER
Green Juice Goody Bags

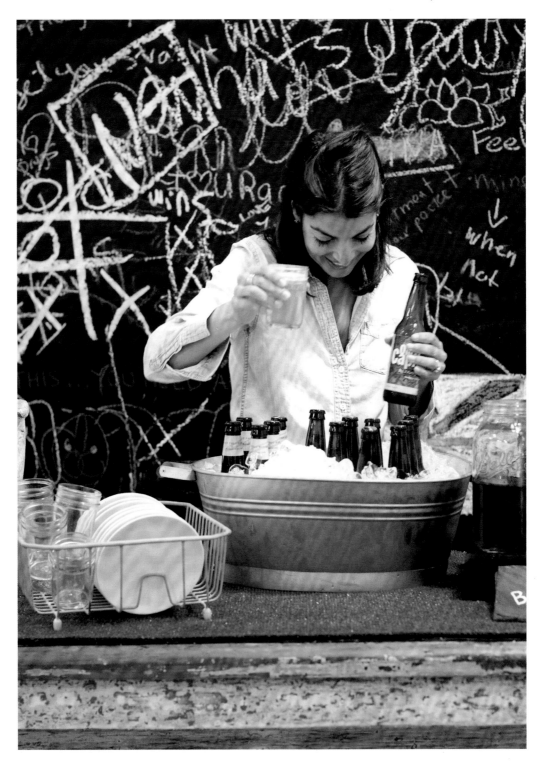

Did you know that Joe Namath once owned a very popular bar named Bachelors III in New York City during the late '60s—early '70s? Talk about one heck of a Cocktail Party! Perhaps Joe was the person who tied game watching and parties together, because it was around that time that watching a sporting event while eating and drinking began to go hand in hand.

Super Bowl or Game Day entertaining is a refreshingly pressure-free party. This is one occasion where you can get messy, offer foods that *will* get your guests' hands dirty, and I encourage you to serve dessert out of mismatched coffee mugs or fill a football helmet with chips. Plus, each week you can seek menu inspiration from the battling teams, which gives you ample opportunity to tie in unique flavors and bites from different regions around the country.

It's also one of those entertaining days where decadence is expected, so make sure your Snacktivities include all kinds of unique toppings. Sometimes by creating comfort hybrids, you can stumble on culinary genius. The Mini Buffalo Chicken Grilled Cheese is one of my favorite examples of this, as is the MACO—a recipe that came to life when I filled a taco shell with leftover mac and cheese, topped it with guacamole, and BOOM . . . MAGIC!

So don't be afraid to top that chili, deck that dog, and dress up that mac. The cheesier, the better, when it comes to Game Day!

Love,
Mary

MINI BUFFALO CHICKEN GRILLED CHEESE

This recipe is a perfect example of combining two iconic foods into one great sandwich. I had the pleasure of making this sandwich with The Barefoot Contessa herself (Ina Garten) on her show. When we were done shooting, we toasted cheers with our mini sandwiches.

YIELD: 24 MINI GRILLED CHEESE
PREP TIME: 10 MINUTES • COOK TIME: 5 TO 10 MINUTES

6 slices soft white bread

2 tablespoons unsalted butter, melted

3 tablespoons crumbled blue cheese, at room temperature

3 teaspoons heavy cream

¾ cup shredded cooked chicken breast

3 tablespoons hot sauce

3 slices pepper Jack cheese

1. Working with 3 pieces of bread, brush both sides of each slice with melted butter.

2. Combine the blue cheese and heavy cream in a small bowl and stir. Spread the mixture on one side of each slice of bread.

3. In a small bowl, mix together the chicken and hot sauce and arrange it over the blue cheese mixture. Place the pepper Jack cheese on top of the chicken and cover it with the other 3 slices of bread.

4. Heat a griddle on top of the stove over medium high heat. Place the sandwiches on the griddle and grill for about 2 to 3 minutes on each side, or until the bread is golden brown and the cheese is melted. Slice the sandwiches into 8 small serving pieces.

5. Serve on a decorative platter with toothpicks or as a passed item on a decorative tray.

MACO (MAC AND CHEESE TACO) WITH GUACAMOLE

8 soft corn tortillas (6-inch)

2 tablespoons olive oil

1 teaspoon salt

black pepper

½ box elbow pasta

3 teaspoons canola oil

1 to 1½ cups whole milk or half-and-half

½ cup diced Velveeta cheese

1 cup TOTAL diced or shredded Gruyère, sharp Cheddar, and fontina cheeses

¼ cup crumbled blue cheese

¼ cup grated Parmesan cheese

1 teaspoon chipotle pepper puree in adobo (available in the ethnic foods aisle of the supermarket)

½ cup guacamole

If you are short on time, Tostitos Scoops work great with this recipe.

YIELD: 24 TACOS
PREP AND COOK TIME: 40 MINUTES TOTAL

1. Preheat the oven to 375°F.

2. Cut out 2.5-inch circles from the tortillas (yields 3 per tortilla).

3. Brush the circles with olive oil on both sides.

4. Place the tortilla circles in mini muffin pans. Sprinkle with salt and pepper and bake until golden, approximately 6 minutes. Let the shells cool. Cover them in an airtight container until ready to use.

5. In a medium pot on high heat, bring 3 quarts of water to a boil. Add a generous pinch of salt to flavor the pasta. Add the pasta, stir, and simmer for approximately 8 minutes, or according to the directions on the package. Once the pasta is cooked, drain into a colander, then lay it out flat in a shallow pan to cool down to room temperature, about 10 minutes.

6. Add the canola oil and stir it through the pasta to avoid clumps.

7. Fill a medium pot one-third of the way up with water. Place a larger stainless bowl over the pot; set on medium. Add the milk or half-and-half and allow it to heat up. Add the cheeses in handfuls and stir with a wooden spoon, until all the cheeses are melted. Check the consistency. If it is too thin and won't stick to the pasta, add more cheese. Add a bit more milk if it appears to be too thick.

8. Stir in the teaspoon of chipotle puree, add salt, and adjust seasonings if needed. Add the pasta. Stir to heat through.

9. Spoon the macaroni into the mini taco shells and garnish with guacamole and additional chipotle puree on top.

10. Serve on a decorative platter (be sure not to set out too early, as tacos shells may get soggy) or pass as a small bite.

BANOFFEE CREAM PIE IN A MUG

I love my mug collection. So much so that I started to serve desserts in mugs, just to show them off more. Game day is a great day to fill up mugs with all sorts of delcious sweet combos. Ice cream with lots of topppings served in mugs is a winner, too. I also use my staircase as my dessert buffet. They're there, might as well use them! These can be made ahead and refrigerated until your guests arrive.

YIELD: 12 COFFEE-MUG PIES
PREP TIME: 2½ HOURS • ASSEMBLY TIME: 10 MINUTES

1. Place the can of sweetened condensed milk in a small pot and cover with water. Bring to a simmer. Simmer for 2½ hours, making sure the can is always covered with water. Let cool.

2. Mix the butter with the crushed graham crackers and cinnamon. Set aside.

3. Whip the heavy cream with the confectioners' sugar and a pinch of salt just until stiff peaks form.

4. Sprinkle a thin layer of the graham cracker mixture into each coffee mug.

5. Top with a layer of caramelized milk, then a layer of banana slices, and whipped cream, each layer approximately ½ inch deep. Repeat until you reach the top of the mug.

6. Garnish with grated dark chocolate and cinnamon.

1 14-ounce can sweetened condensed milk

6 tablespoons unsalted butter, melted

1½ cups crushed graham crackers

2 teaspoons ground cinnamon, plus extra for garnish

1 pint heavy whipping cream

1 tablespoon confectioners' sugar

Pinch of salt

2 large ripe bananas, sliced

Dark chocolate, for grating

"CHOPRETZATO" (CHOCOLATE, PRETZEL, POTATO CHIP PUDDING IN A MUG)

2 3.9-ounce boxes chocolate pudding mix

4 cups whole or low-fat milk

1 pint heavy whipping cream

1 tablespoon confectioners' sugar

Salt

1 cup salted mini pretzels, crushed

1 cup salted potato chips, crushed

Dark chocolate, for grating

YIELD: 12 COFFEE-MUG CONFECTIONS
PREP TIME: 15 MINUTES

1. Prepare chocolate pudding according to the package directions, using the milk. Chill and let set.

2. Whip the heavy cream with the confectioners' sugar and a pinch of salt just until stiff peaks form.

3. Put the pretzels in a ziplock bag and crush them into bite-size pieces.

4. Repeat the process with the potato chips.

5. Sprinkle a thin layer of the pretzel crumbs in each coffee mug.

6. Top with a layer of chocolate pudding, then a layer of crushed potato chips, and then whipped cream. Repeat until you reach the top of the mug.

7. Garnish with a sprinkling of pretzels and potato chips and some grated dark chocolate.

Party Prep Playlist

"Superbowl Shuffle" (The Chicago Bears), "Start Me Up" (The Rolling Stones), "The Divide" (Grace Potter & the Nocturnals), "We Will Rock You" (Queen), "Centerfield" (John Fogerty), "Eye of the Tiger" (Survivor), "Hungry Like the Wolf" (Duran Duran), "Dead or Alive" (Bon Jovi), "Sam's Town" (The Killers), "Crazy Train" (Ozzy Osbourne), "Rock Child" (Pearl Aday), "Pyromania" (Def Leppard), "Gimme Shelter" (The Rolling Stones), "All Along the Watchtower" (Jimi Hendrix)

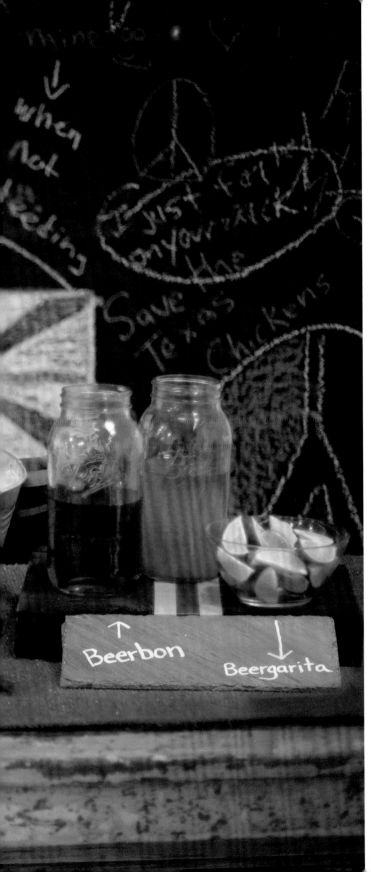

It's Game Day, so we might as well play with our beer. I suggest filling an ice tub with beers and then have the bourbon and the margarita mix (recipe below) on hand to mix in. Gives your guests a chance to make a home-run cocktail.

BEERBON

YIELD: 12 SERVINGS

12 12-ounce cans of beer

1 24-ounce bottle of your favorite bourbon

You can either pour the ingredients into a drink receptacle and serve OR serve the beers in a beer tub with a bottle of bourbon and encourage your guests to mix together.

BEERGARITA

YIELD: 12 SERVINGS

12 12-ounce cans of beer

12 ounces tequila

12 ounces fresh lime juice

Carefully combine the ingredients and gently stir (do *not* shake, as the beer will get too frothy). Serve in Margarita glasses.

This is the perfect day to break out a galvanized tub or drink cooler. Just make sure you have a few openers handy.

DRESS YOUR PIGS IN A BLANKET

Homemade pigs in a blanket are great, but they are time-consuming to make from scratch, and with a brush of melted butter, you can make the frozen ones taste homemade.

- *Buy 4 dozen frozen pigs in a blanket.*

- *Set out in a single layer on greased baking sheets.*

- *Melt 2 tablespoons of butter, brush on the pigs, and bake according to the package instructions.*

- *Arrange the pigs on cake stands. Pigs in a blanket are great served warm, but are also delicious at room temp.*

- *Set out unique toppings like guacamole, hot sauce, mustards, ketchup, bbq sauce, relish, sauerkraut, crumbled bacon, and blue cheese in 4-inch bowls.*

- *Sauces can be served in mini squeeze bottles or in 4-inch bowls.*

- *Small plates and napkins are all that is required for this one.*

HARD
&
BE NICE
TO PEOPLE

DIY GRILLED CHEESE BAR

It's game time! Astroturf makes for an inexpensive and festive runner or tablecloth. (You can purchase it at any Home Depot or hardware store.)

- *Always set the snacktivity station in order of preparation:*

  1. Breads (white, rye, whole wheat)

  2. Spreads (butter, mustard, mayo, olive oil, blue cheese spread)

  3. Cheeses (Cheddar, American, Muenster, and pepper Jack)

  4. Fillings (bacon, chicken, grilled veggies, pastrami, turkey, chili)

- *Grill. You can use a grill (as shown) or a* *plug-in panini maker or grilled cheese maker. Whatever you use, make sure you set it to a medium temperature.*

- *Fill up a helmet with your favorite chips and pickles. You can't have a grilled cheese without chips and a pickle.*

Another fun Snacktivity is the DIY Indoor Hot Dog Tailgate. Use a mini bbq (Weber makes great ones), and you can re-create the tailgate experience at home. Pre-grill the hot dogs and use the mini bbq as a display, set out with lots of yummy toppings.

Green Juice Goody Bags

There is a lot of indulgent stuff on this menu! So be a thoughtful host and send your guests home with all the makings for a healthy juice the next morning. Fill a paper bag with a small bunch of kale or spinach, one green apple, two sliced lemon wedges, and a small baggie filled with 1 teaspoon of cayenne pepper. All your guests will have to do is throw this in the blender or juicer the next morning and let the cleanse begin!

cayenne

THAT TIME I SPILLED SEA BASS ON KEANU REEVES

As I mentioned earlier, I am not much of a sports gal, nor do I partake in the activity of sports watching. And while I'm very proud to say that I've catered an event for the New York Jets where Joe Namath was present, other than once attending a bat mitzvah where Jimmy Connors was signing tennis balls, that's all I got in the sports department.

Actually, that's not true; I did once pull a very sportsmanlike maneuver with our waiters to remove an offending piece of sea bass that had accidently fallen onto Keanu Reeves's jacket while we were French-serving a dinner at The Woodstock Film Festival. My captain (literally, my service captain, Chris) was the offensive coordinator, alerting me to the fallen piece of fish. My server Shawn, as quarterback, did a hand-off of a service napkin to me, playing the role of the running back, so that I could travel through the party with stealthlike precision. But . . . dammit!! interception from Vera Farmiga, who leaned in to chat with Keanu. Finally, after a short time-out, I approached Neo, I mean Keanu, and casually placed my hand with the napkin on his sleeve, asking if I could get him anything from the bar. Touchdown . . . I think? Either way, crisis averted.

And since I'm a good sport (ha ha ha), I don't want to leave any sports fans/party enthusiasts out in the cold, so I've decided to consult a glossary of sports terms that you can apply toward your next party. I'll pretend I'm your captain (which is funny coming from a girl who joined cross country just so she could run past the players at football practice in short shorts and a cropped tank top), but let's go with it.

You are the QUARTERBACK of your party; you set the tone, look, feel, smell, mood, and time for your event. You are in control and have to read the players and are aware of their moves, even if it's just steering them in the direction of the bathroom.

KEEP YOUR EYE ON THE BALL. Anticipate your guests' needs before they ask; have drinks ready when they arrive; have snacks set out for nibbling; have a delicious scented candle and hand towels in the bathroom; know when to serve dessert and when to say good night. You always want to end the party with your guests wanting more.

You will be grateful to have RECEIVERS to enjoy all the hard work, planning, love and efforts.

There may be INTERCEPTIONS: an unexpected guest of a guest, a burnt cake, a spilled glass of wine, or a late arrival. Be all that you can be (oh, wait, I think that's the Army slogan). Just go with the flow. Don't sweat the small stuff; have a "more is more" or shake-it-off attitude.

Your first GOAL will be very rewarding; whether it be a compliment on your cheese platter, a "Hey! Best cocktail ever!" remark, or perhaps even the ultimate may occur—an impromptu dance party erupts. This is a moment when you can SPIKE your vodka . . . again . . . in celebration.

If a FULL COURT PRESS moment occurs (party conversation becomes a little too heavy, debates erupt, your drunk neighbor mistakes your dog for his wife's coat), time to confetti bomb the crap out of everyone.

HAIL MARY: Something I do before all parties and after my guests leave.

PUNCH DRUNK: A boxing term and also the objective of your punch bowl.

Don't get SUCKER PUNCHED by a difficult guest. It's okay if you don't have chamomile tea or if the meat you're serving isn't grass-fed. Have pride in what you chose to serve, don't apologize. A guest once asked me (after I had set up a beautiful party) if I had a bag of sand and some rocks!? While I usually pride myself on being a prepared hostess, there are just some requests you won't be able to fulfill. I still have no idea what he wanted them for.

VICTORY LAP: When your guests call or email to offer their thanks, don't waste time telling them you wished the steaks were less well done or that the whipped cream had more airy peaks. Odds are no one noticed anything amiss but you, so THREE CHEERS FOR THE HOME TEAM!

The less you fret about winning their hearts, minds, and stomachs, the more they'll love you . . . and if they don't, please refer to PUNCH DRUNK.

CHAPTER 5

Awards Season

EAT
Edamame Dumplings

Chicken Satay

Banana, Mango, and Chocolate Spring Rolls

Champagne Jell-O

DRINK
Easiest Champagne Drink Ever

Buddha Punch

PLAY
Coffee Table Pupu Platter

Best-Dressed Chips

Punch Drunk Bowls

RECOVER
Swag Bag Goodie Bags

I am very grateful that my company has had the opportunity to cater many exciting film premieres. Nothing jazzes me more than when we are tasked to come up with creative food, drink, and décor ideas inspired by a particular film or television show. Awards-show viewing parties offer you the exact same opportunity. When thinking about your Viewing Party (or Movie Night Party), the Cocktail Party formula is perfect.

Look at the list of Best Picture nominees and choose small bites inspired by the various films, choose snacktivities that are coffee table—friendly so your guests don't miss a single envelope, and theme up those drinks. Thanks to *The Big Lebowski* The Dude turned us on to White Russians again—and an even bigger thanks to *The Jerk,* for introducing us to Pizza in a Cup!

Or . . . Do what I do on Oscar Night and "Honor the Vics"—Trader Vic's, that is. In the '60s, Trader Vic's was *the* spot to watch the Oscars, so I celebrate this Hollywood tradition by ordering in for my Oscar Party. Therefore, I hereby grant you permission to dust off that pupu platter (or buy a new one on eBay), shake up a pitcher of mai tais, and order out, because tonight is the best night of the year to "act" like you cooked the entire meal.

Love,
Mary

EDAMAME DUMPLINGS

Remember, you can always just order 24 assorted dumplings from your favorite Chinese take-out place.

YIELD: 24 DUMPLINGS
PREP TIME: 25 MINUTES • COOK TIME: 15 MINUTES

Dipping Sauce

- 2 scallions, thinly chopped
- 2 tablespoons soy sauce
- 1 teaspoon honey
- Pinch of red pepper flakes

Dumplings

- 1 cup frozen shelled edamame
- 2 tablespoons sesame oil
- 2 teaspoons minced fresh ginger
- 1 garlic clove, minced
- Juice of 1 lemon
- 1 egg white
- 1 teaspoon sriracha or other hot sauce
- 1 teaspoon tamari or soy sauce
- 24 wonton wrappers
- ¼ cup vegetable oil, for pan frying

1. For the Dipping Sauce: Add all the ingredients in a bowl and mix well; set aside.

2. For the Dumplings: Cook the edamame according to the package directions, drain and cool. In a food processor, add the edamame, sesame oil, ginger, garlic, lemon juice, egg white, hot sauce, and tamari. Process until smooth.

3. Place a teaspoon of filling in the center of each wonton. Brush the outer edges with water to help seal the dough. Fold the opposite corners to seal each one like a triangle. Pinch all the edges to seal. Place on a tray with a damp towel to keep them from drying out.

4. Fill a frying pan with the vegetable oil and heat until warm. Pan fry the dumplings on each side until golden brown.

5. Serve with the dipping sauce on the side.

6. Serve on a decorative platter or as part of a snacktivity Pupu Platter.

CHICKEN SATAY

This one is always a welcome crowd pleaser.

Spicy Peanut Sauce

- 1 cup unsalted dry-roasted peanuts
- ⅓ cup coconut milk
- ⅓ cup sweet chili glaze (can be found in the supermarket)
- 2 teaspoons chopped fresh cilantro
- Juice of 1 lime
- 1 teaspoon peanut butter
- 1 garlic clove, minced
- 1 teaspoon Asian fish sauce
- 1 teaspoon chili paste

Marinade

- ¼ cup fresh lime juice
- 1 stalk lemongrass, minced
- 3 garlic cloves, minced
- 1 fresh red chili (or bird's eye chili) sliced thin
- 2 teaspoons Asian fish sauce
- 2 teaspoons dark brown sugar
- 1 teaspoon soy sauce
- 1 teaspoon minced fresh ginger
- ½ teaspoon sesame oil
- ½ teaspoon dried turmeric
- 1½ pounds boneless, skinless chicken breasts

YIELD: 24 SKEWERS
PREP TIME: 3 HOURS • COOK TIME: 6 MINUTES

1. Soak 24 bamboo skewers in cold water for at least 30 minutes or metal skewers may be used and do not have to be soaked first.

2. For the Peanut Sauce: Combine the peanuts, coconut milk, chili glaze, cilantro, lime juice, peanut butter, garlic, fish sauce, and chili paste in a blender or food processor and purée. Thin the purée by adding more coconut milk if needed. To increase the saltiness, add more fish sauce in small dashes.

3. For the Marinade: In a medium-size bowl, whisk together the lime juice, lemongrass, garlic, chili, fish sauce, sugar, soy sauce, ginger, sesame oil, and turmeric.

4. Slice the chicken into even strips the width of a finger, about 3 inches long. Add chicken to the marinade and stir to coat. Cover with plastic wrap and refrigerate for about 2½ hours.

5. Preheat a grill on medium-high. Remove the chicken from the refrigerator and drain out the liquid.

6. Skewer each piece of chicken and grill on both sides until cooked through, about 3 minutes per side.

7. Serve hot with the peanut sauce on the side for dipping.

8. Serve on a decorative platter or as part of a snacktivity Pupu Platter.

BANANA, MANGO, AND CHOCOLATE SPRING ROLLS

Fried bananas, mango, and chocolate in one crispy bite. You serve this, and I guarantee the next time you send out a party invite, those RSVPs will roll in faster than you can say Banana, Mango, and Chocolate Spring Rolls.

YIELD: 24 SPRING ROLLS
PREP TIME: 20 MINUTES • COOK TIME: 10 MINUTES

12 spring roll wrappers

3 bananas, peeled and halved lengthwise and crosswise to make 8 pieces per banana

2 mangoes, peeled and pitted, cut lengthwise into 3 x ½-inch strips

6 tablespoons chopped candied ginger

6 tablespoons chocolate chips

1 egg, beaten

1 quart vegetable oil

Salt

1. Line a baking sheet with parchment paper. Place 1 spring roll wrapper on the counter so that it is in a diamond shape. Place 1 banana piece, 1 mango strip, 1 teaspoon of chopped candied ginger, and 1 teaspoon of chocolate chips across the center of each wrap.

2. Fold the bottom corner of the wrapper up to the top corner to cover the fruit, making a triangle. Brush the top of the wrapper with the beaten egg. Fold the sides in and roll up to complete the spring roll. Place on the prepared baking sheet and repeat for the remaining spring rolls.

3. Pour the vegetable oil into a deep skillet or heavy-bottomed pot. Heat the oil to 350°F. Working in batches, add the spring rolls to the oil and cook until golden and crisp, turning often. Using a slotted spoon, transfer to paper towels to drain and sprinkle with salt.

4. To finish, cut each spring roll in half on the bias and serve warm.

5. Serve on a decorative platter or as part of a snacktivity Pupu Platter.

CHAMPAGNE JELL-O

2 cups raspberry soda or raspberry seltzer

1 3-ounce box unflavored gelatin

1½ cups champagne

½ cup Chambord or raspberry vodka, for stronger shot

Colored sugars or edible gold (optional, for garnish)

YIELD: 8 TO 10 SERVINGS

PREP TIME: 10 MINUTES • CHILLING TIME: 3 TO 4 HOURS

1. In a saucepan, bring the soda to a boil. Remove from the heat and sprinkle the gelatin over the hot liquid and stir to mix in. Let sit until dissolved, about 2 minutes. Let cool to room temperature.

2. In a mixing bowl combine the gelatin, champagne, and Chambord. Let chill at least 3 hours.

3. When set, scoop into small bowls for serving and sprinkle with the colored sugars or edible gold to give it a little extra sparkle.

Party Prep Playlist

"Arthur's Theme" (Christopher Cross), "Ain't That a Kick in the Head" (Dean Martin), "Theme from E.T." (John Williams), "Jaws Theme" (John Williams), "You've Got a Friend in Me" (Randy Newman), "Porpoise Song" (The Monkees), "So Far So Good" (Sheena Easton), "Oh Yeah" (Yello, Ferris Bueller's Day Off Soundtrack), "Home" (David Byrne), "Rags to Riches" (Tony Bennett), "Layla" (Eric Clapton), "And When She Danced" (David Foster), "Tiny Dancer" (Elton John), "Moon River" (Andy Williams), "Rainbow Connection" (Kermit), "Speak Softly, Love" (Theme from The Godfather), "Norwegian Wood" (The Beatles)

SUBWAY BRUCE DAVIDSON

WALKER

The Negative   ADAMS   2

Polaroid Land Photography   ADAMS

TASCHEN

THE ROCK 'N' ROLL PHOTOGRAPHY
OF KEN REGAN

EASIEST CHAMPAGNE DRINK EVER

And the best-dressed champagne glass goes to . . . this recipe. It's chic, it's easy, and it looks pretty in your bowl and in your glass.

YIELD: 10 TO 12 SERVINGS

- 4 bottles champagne (or prosecco, which is cheaper and bubbles will last longer)
- 1 bottle raspberry flavored seltzer
- 2 cups fresh raspberries

Pour the champagne and seltzer into a punch bowl and serve in fluted white wine glasses with ice and raspberries.

BUDDHA PUNCH

This comes from Robert and Anne London's Cocktails & Snacks (*1965*).

YIELD: 10 TO 12 SERVINGS

- 1 bottle dry, slightly fruity white wine
- 6 ounces orange juice
- 6 ounces lemon juice
- 3 ounces triple sec
- 3 ounces rum
- 1 bottle champagne (or prosecco)
- 2 1-liter bottles club soda

    Lemon and orange slices, pineapple chunks, fresh mint for garnish

    Dash of bitters (can be purchased at the supermarket or your liquor store; my favorite brand is Angostura.)

Mix together the wine, orange juice, lemon juice, triple sec, and rum. Pour over a block of ice in a punch bowl. Just before serving, add the champagne and soda. Garnish with small slices of lemon, orange, pineapple, and fresh mint. Add a dash of bitters to taste.

COFFEE TABLE PUPU PLATTER

Use an actual pupu platter or lazy Susan with dishes (shown in picture) to re-create the real pupu experience.

- *Make sure you have enough plates for the items you order.*

- *Easy Chinese takeout (for 10 to 12 people):*

  - *2 quart-size containers boneless spareribs (you'll have extra, but they taste like candy if you eat them cold the next day)*

  - *12 egg rolls (cut in half to make 24 pieces)*

  - *24 pieces chicken satay (if you didn't go for the homemade)*

  - *24 assorted dumplings (if you didn't go for the homemade)*

- *Set out individual sauce bowls for each person (duck, soy, spicy mustard, peanut).*

- *There are three times to use wet wipes—clambakes, bbq, and pupu platter—so use 'em if you have 'em.*

- *When ordering takeout, ask for additional containers, so you can ditch the plates for these instead and then your guests can take home their leftovers.*

- *Later, serve a dessert that is coffee table–friendly, like chocolate fondue, so guests can enjoy it without missing the last envelope opening.*

tortilla chips

spicy salsa

BEST-DRESSED CHIPS

Take your average chips and dips and give them the red carpet treatment. Set out assorted chips with protein toppings (in separate 4-inch bowls), like chicken and beans; spreads like spicy guacamole, ranch dressing, and mango salsa; and toppings like crumbled bacon, sliced jalapeños, and fried onions. *Voilà!* The award for the best-dressed chip goes to . . .

potato chips

crackers

shredded pork

black bean dip

black bean salsa

ranch dressing

bacon

shredded chicken

PUNCH DRUNK BOWLS

Awards and viewing parties are a great time to use your punch bowl, especially since the drinks I'm suggesting are Polynesian-ish.

- *Also, the use of a punch bowl makes your party bartender-free.*

- *I love a glass punch bowl, so you can see all the yummy fruit floating around. There are lots of edible flowers available now, too, and those make a pretty addition to your punch.*

- *Make sure you have the proper amount of glasses set next to the bowl. There won't be a lot of up and down during this party, so one glass per guest should do.*

- *Long gone are the days of watered-down punches, because there are great stone cubes that you can freeze and use to keep your punch cold without getting watery. (Crate & Barrel and Bed Bath & Beyond carry them.)*

- *A nice runner underneath the bowl and glasses looks decorative and catches spills.*

Swag Bag Goodie Bags

Send your guests home with their very own bags of swag and pampering favors, so they can do what all the stars do after the Oscars . . . SPA.

love, mary

le soap

Fill a mason jar with nail polish, nail file, lavender soap, and a face mask.

THE NIGHT JACK HAD TO USE THE JOHN

As I grew older and my dreams of winning an Oscar dissipated, I replaced them with the desire to cater to the stars in Hollywood someday. New York has been very good to me, but Los Angeles, as it was when I was a young girl watching the Oscars, was the prize I had my eye on.

Last year (after almost ten years in business), Hollywood finally did come calling. We were asked to cater an extremely VIP dinner during Oscars week and the dream and the reality became, well, one of the hardest days of my *entire* career. It went a little something like this . . .

4:00 a.m. Woken and told that our chef had a fever and probably the flu and would not be able to leave his bed, let alone cook for the A-list of A-listers we were serving that evening.

7:00 a.m. I put my sneakers and apron on and join John (our chef assistant) in kitchen triage. I had no idea whether or not John could cook an egg, let alone dinner for Hollywood's A-list.

7:01 a.m. Realize Chef John is a rock star and that I am lucky to be in the same kitchen with him.

11:30 a.m. Get a call that two of the waiters have canceled.

12:30 p.m. Peel boiled beets without gloves (won't do that again).

2:00 p.m. Run out to get mixers for the bar, get pulled over by LAPD for making a U-turn . . . tears topped with "I'm from New York" get me out of a ticket.

4:00 p.m. Chef John and team leave for the party; I agree to stay behind and wait for the ice cream to set. Tonight's flavor (toasted marshmallow) is a special recipe passed on by Chef Pascal Tingaud (Executive Chef for Dom Pérignon) that was to be paired with the 1983 Vintage Dom we were pouring that evening at dessert. This dessert is *the most important part* of the meal.

7 p.m. Apply heels and dress and check on the ice cream. It's a soupy glob that does not resemble ice cream in any way.

7:30 p.m. Panic and wake up sleeping Chef Matt (the one with the fever and flu) and ask what we should do. I'm sent to the SLS Hotel and assured they can help us with their very fancy new ice cream maker.

8:15 p.m. Arrive at the back door of the Hotel SLS in heels, carrying the cooler (you would have thought there was an organ in there) and yelling, "I need [hotel manager] Gustavo!" kinda like Shirley MacLaine yelling at the nurse in *Terms of Endearment* that it was time for her daughter's shot.

8:15–8:30 p.m. I complete twenty-six Hail Marys and grab a smoke with the dishwashers (promise, I haven't smoked in a long time), contemplate early retirement and how unglamorous and superstressful it is to serve the superfamous.

9 p.m. Arrive at the party, running down Melrose Place with my heart, I mean, ice cream in a cooler, and hand it off to Sean, our head captain.

9:15 p.m. Ice cream is served . . . crisis averted, party is moving along nicely.

At around 11 p.m., once I finally declared we would work in this town again, I stepped outside the kitchen to steal a peek at the room of forty-plus all-time A-list celebs sitting at a table beautiful enough to be in a movie, laughing, clinking glasses, and having a great time.

Broken, exhausted, tired, feet bleeding, hands stained with beets, and realizing I had been awake for twenty hours, I hear a familiar voice say, "I gotta use the john."

Sure enough, I turn around and it's Jack . . . as in Nicholson.

Here we are in a small hallway between the kitchen and the bathroom . . . just me and Jack.

I grin from ear to ear (it's JACK!!!!) and he stops (for a second) and smiles and says, "You look like a really happy girl." And then he walked away.

And I guess I was, because I had dreamt to make it to Hollywood someday and I did, albeit not in the way I had planned. But Jack's acknowledging my happiness for a job well done, observing my sense of fulfillment from doing what I love even on the toughest days, was as good as him handing me that gold statuette.

So, thanks for that special moment, Jack. Even though you were just headed to "use the john," you gave me a sparkle of that Hollywood magic I've always dreamt of . . . and now, if I may, I'd like to thank the Academy.

GUESS WHO'S *NOT* COMING TO DINNER

Some people may dream of a taking a fantasy vacation, buying a new car, being a contestant on *The Price Is Right*. Well, my dream is hosting a Cocktail Party for people (dead or alive) in my Woodstock Party Barn. The list changes up every once in a while, but below is my absolute dream list. Who's on yours?

MY DREAM PARTY GUEST LIST

#1 invite . . . **Mickey Dolenz** from The Monkees. Let's face it folks, I am about five minutes away from either having a cardboard cutout of Mickey permanently seated at our dinner table, or being committed. Hmm . . . that's a fun party idea. Straitjackets and finger food?

Next up . . . **Rip Taylor**. Remember that guy from the '70s game shows who would toss confetti all over himself? I just think it would be great to have a guest at the dinner table who would sporadically do that.

Lucille Ball. A) 'Cause I think she is amazing. B) 'Cause I heard she drank like a man.

Steve Martin—but only if he agreed to play the banjo and sing "The Thermos Song" from *The Jerk*.

Gilda Radner. Would love to just sit on my back porch, look at the stars, and laugh with her.

So then I guess if we had Gilda, I'd love **Lorne Michaels** and the cast of SNL to come along too, from 1975–79 and 1984–85, so I could do the Ed Grimley dance with Martin Short between the second and third courses.

Chuck Barris, but only if he brought his gong. I am really thinking about having a *Gong Show* brunch this summer. How fun would that be, to invite all your pals over to perform, eat bagels, and then gong them?

Did I mention that **Mario Batali** was cooking for us and **Salvador Dalí** would assist as his sous chef?

Brad and Angelina—not because of the obvious, but because I figure they have so many kids, chances are high after a few too many of my jalapeño-grapefruit margaritas, they may leave one behind, and then, "POOF!" Ryan and I have an instant family.

Carole Demas and Paula Janis, the ladies from *The Magic Garden*. Could be fun to bring them out for dessert to sing a song and serve a Chuckle Patch dessert garden. (We created this dessert for a client recently—Sweet 'Shrooms and Berries.) However, I'm just not sure if I would want them to stick around, post-song. I guess I could ask Rip Taylor to confetti-bomb them and shoo them out the door.

The Captain and Tennille. I'm imagining that they would warm up to us rather quickly and at the end of the night, The Captain would give Ryan his hat as a symbol of his gratitude, and, going forward, whenever Ryan was asked, "Where did you get that hat?" he could respond, "The Captain." And if they asked, "Which Captain?" Ryan would chuckle and say, "Is there any other Captain?"

After dessert, **George Takei** would

suggest a game of charades and I would find myself conflicted if I should team up with **ET** (the alien) or **Janis Joplin**.

And how great would it be if, around midnight, **Dean Martin** and **Frank Sinatra** stumbled into the barn, smelling of Scotch and cigarettes, asking first to use the john and second if I'd be a doll and freshen their cocktails while they "see a man about a dog."

And then, finally, Ryan would have to help me get everyone out 'cause he knows we have to prepare for our brunch guests the next morning. Yup, you guessed it . . . **Liza Minnelli** and **Joan Rivers**.

Who's on *your* dream party guest list???

CHAPTER 6

Surprise Party

EAT

Mac and Cheese Cupcakes

Pastrami Sandwich Muffins

Sweet Arancini (Rice Balls)

Mixed Berry Pizza

DRINK

Tequila Cosmo

Wine-garita

PLAY

Savory Waffles Bar, aka Night Waffles

Savory Vodka Bar

RECOVER

Cleanup Supply List to Cover All Party Surprises

A surprise party can be a *really* good idea or a *really* bad one. This is why I always advise my clients to consider, instead of throwing a surprise party (where they run the risk of giving Uncle Howard a heart attack), adding *an element of surprise* to their event. This keeps home entertaining from becoming stale for the guests as well as the host.

Start with the location . . .

Don't assume you can serve food only from an actual kitchen. I have served some fancy people from some less-than-fancy locales, like Gwyneth Paltrow's bushes, Jerry Seinfeld's garage, the copy room of *Vogue* magazine (literally on the copy machine . . . picture Judy in the movie *Nine to Five* meets Ina Garten), and, one time, out of the coat closet of a famous CEO's house (just me and a convection oven smushed between his ski jacket and tennis bag). When my clients ask, "Can we do the party here?" I always respond, "Where there's a plug, there's a way!"

Now how about food and drink . . .

Let's take things we're used to being savory and make them sweet, serve dinner in our pajamas, and make margaritas out of wine!? Why not? Who's stopping you? Not me.

Love,
Mary

MAC AND CHEESE CUPCAKES

Kids, grandparents, dogs, babies . . . they all love these cupcake-shaped bites. Easy and delicious, with lots of fun toppings; a great bite that your party guests can customize to their liking. If you want some healthier variations, try subbing in whole wheat pasta or Annie's Mac & Cheese (rather than Kraft) and add some fresh spinach and fontina to the mixture before you place it into the cupcake tins.

2 7.25-ounce boxes store-bought mac and cheese or your favorite homemade recipe, yielding 4 cups of mac and cheese

1 tablespoon hot sauce

½ cup shredded Cheddar cheese

½ cup shredded Gruyère cheese

½ cup of each item to be used as a topping: truffle oil, hot sauce, chopped bacon, and scallions

YIELD: 24 CUPCAKES
PREP TIME: 15 MINUTES • COOK TIME: 40 MINUTES

1. Preheat the oven to 350°F.

2. Make mac and cheese according to the instructions on the package. Once cooked, stir in the hot sauce and shredded cheeses.

3. Oil two 12-cup mini muffin pans.

4. Scoop the mac and cheese mixture into the prepped mini muffin pans and bake for 15 to 40 minutes, or until the tops are golden brown.

5. Serve on a platter with the toppings in bowls so guests can customize their bites.

PASTRAMI SANDWICH MUFFINS

I am a big fan of Jewish cuisine, so much so that I was asked to contribute to a book called Eating Delancey: A Celebration of Jewish Food, *where I wrote about my deep love for Katz's deli—specifically their pastrami. I warn you these will go fast, so maybe make a few extra for yourself and set aside until after your party guests leave.*

YIELD: 24 SANDWICH MUFFINS
PREP TIME: 20 MINUTES • COOK TIME: 15 MINUTES

2 teaspoons caraway seeds

2 cups all-purpose flour

4 teaspoons sugar

2 teaspoons baking powder

½ teaspoon salt

2 eggs

1 cup milk

4 tablespoons (½ stick) unsalted butter, melted

⅓ cup shredded Gruyère cheese (plus additional for serving)

½ cup sauerkraut, drained

½ pound pastrami, diced in ¼-inch pieces

Your favorite mustard(s)

1. Preheat the oven to 375°F.

2. In a dry pan on low heat, toast the caraway seeds until fragrant, shaking the pan for even toastiness. This happens quickly, so don't leave the pan and wander off.

3. In a small bowl, combine the flour, sugar, baking powder, salt, and caraway seeds. In another bowl, combine the eggs, milk, and melted butter. Stir the liquids into the dry mix just until combined. Fold in the cheese.

4. Grease 2 mini muffin pans and fill the cups three-quarters of the way.

5. Bake for about 15 minutes, or until a toothpick inserted in the center comes out clean. Place on a wire rack to cool completely before serving.

6. In a small bowl, mix together the sauerkraut and pastrami.

7. Gently warm the sauerkraut and pastrami in a small pot or in the microwave.

8. Split each muffin horizontally about three-quarters of the way across. Carefully open the muffins a little to squeeze in some mustard, then a mound of the sauerkraut and pastrami mix.

9. Serve on a decorative platter or pass as a small bite, with extra cheese.

SWEET ARANCINI (RICE BALLS)

5 cups whole milk

1 cup heavy cream

2 tablespoons unsalted butter

1 cup arborio rice

½ cup dried currants

½ teaspoon ground cinnamon

1 tablespoon lemon zest, plus more for garnish

⅓ cup granulated sugar

½ teaspoon salt

1 quart vegetable oil

¼ cup all-purpose flour

2 eggs, beaten

½ cup graham cracker crumbs

Powdered sugar

Lemon zest

This is a nice unexpected sweet bite. Like a fried rice pudding, which makes me now want to think of a way to fry chocolate pudding . . . hmmm . . . next book.

YIELD: 24 BITE-SIZE RICE BALLS
PREP TIME: 30 MINUTES • COOK TIME: 10 MINUTES

1. Bring the milk and heavy cream to a simmer in a small saucepan. Turn the heat down to the lowest setting to keep warm.

2. Melt the butter in a large saucepan and stir in the rice to coat the grains. Toast the rice lightly for about 3 minutes, until lightly golden. Stir in the currants. Ladle about 1 cup of the warmed milk and cream into the rice mixture and simmer until it is absorbed, stirring frequently over medium heat. Repeat this process until the rice is almost tender. Before the final addition of milk, stir in the cinnamon, lemon zest, sugar, and salt. Continue to cook until all the liquid is absorbed.

3. Remove from the heat and pour the cooked rice out onto a buttered baking sheet to cool completely. When the rice has cooled, roll it into 24 golf ball–size balls.

4. Pour the oil into a heavy-bottomed skillet and heat it to 350°F.

5. Set up the coating ingredients—flour, beaten eggs, and graham cracker crumbs—each in a separate shallow bowl. Roll the arancini first in the flour, then the egg, and then the graham cracker crumbs.

6. Fry the arancini in small batches, flipping to cook evenly until golden brown, about 10 minutes. Remove from the oil and place on a plate lined with paper towels to drain.

7. Top with the powdered sugar and lemon zest and serve on a decorative platter or pass as a small bite.

MIXED BERRY PIZZA

1 5-ounce store-bought pizza dough, thawed

Flour, for work surface

2 cups mascarpone cheese

2 tablespoons honey

1 tablespoon heavy cream

1 teaspoon lemon zest

1 cup blueberries

1 cup blackberries

2 tablespoons chopped fresh mint

2 tablespoons chopped fresh basil

Freshly ground black pepper

My nieces and nephew love this one. Many grocery stores now offer both regular semolina and whole wheat pizza dough. Both would work well here.

YIELD: 24 PIZZA SQUARES
PREP TIME: 15 MINUTES • COOK TIME: 15 MINUTES

1. Preheat the oven to 400°F. Line a baking sheet with parchment paper.

2. Place the pizza dough on a well-floured work surface and shape and stretch the dough with your fingers into a 12 x 8-inch rectangle. Place on the prepared baking sheet and bake for 15 minutes, or until the bottom is golden.

3. While the dough bakes, mix together the mascarpone, honey, cream, and lemon zest.

4. Spread the mascarpone mixture over the pizza and top with the berries, mint, basil, and black pepper.

5. Cut into 24 small squares. Serve on a round pizza tray or display on a cake stand.

Party Prep Playlist

"Baby, What a Big Surprise" (Chicago), "Surprise Surprise" (The Rolling Stones), "That Was Then, This Is Now" (The Monkees), "Abracadabra" (Steve Miller), "Girl You Know It's True" (Milli Vanilli), "Toxic" (Britney Spears), "Nobody Home" (Pink Floyd), "In the Air Tonight" (Phil Collins), "Star Spangled Banner" (Jimi Hendrix), "Shanghai Surprise" (George Harrison), "Goodbye Surprise" (The Turtles)

TEQUILA COSMO

I am a lady who was living in New York in her twenties during the whole Sex and the City *Cosmo phenomenon, so by the year 2010, I needed to find a new drink. I switched the vodka to tequila and WOW—a drink that could easily take me into my forties.*

YIELD: 12 SERVINGS

24 ounces white cranberry juice

12 ounces tequila (Patrón preferred)

12 ounces triple sec

Combine the ingredients in a drink dispenser of your choice. Serve in martini glasses.

WINE-GARITA

Every year, my husband, Ryan, and I take a food-inspiration trip. Last year, we went to Arroyo Seco, a beautiful little town outside of Taos, New Mexico. We found this quaint little restaurant called ACEQ and ordered a pitcher of margaritas. They were the most delicious ones I'd ever had—so good that I had to ask for the recipe. I was so surprised to find out that they made their margaritas with wine instead of tequila. So, no surprise that I ordered another pitcher.

YIELD: 12 SERVINGS

2 bottles white wine (I like a pinot grigio/ gris or Sancerre)

1 cup fresh lime juice

2 quarts orange juice

Combine the ingredients in a drink dispenser of your choice. Serve with ice in rocks or hurricane glasses.

SAVORY WAFFLES BAR, AKA NIGHT WAFFLES

Waffles are no longer for kids. With a savory chickpea waffle batter, you can serve this at your party and surprise your guests with the unexpected deliciousness. Savory-flavored waffles can now be found in the freezer section of most high-end supermarkets. If you want to tackle making your own, I encourage you to do so.

- *I suggest making the waffles in advance and then heating and displaying them shortly before guests arrive.*

- *Set out toppings in tagines (Pier One, Crate & Barrel, and HomeGoods have great tagines): tzatziki sauce, hot sauce, feta cheese dip, sliced cucumbers, tomatoes, onions, tandoori spiced chicken, and chicken saag (either take-out or homemade).*

- *Small plates and forks are all you will need.*

- *Get festive with your napkins. A unique fabric could be purchased at your local fabric store and cut down into individual cocktail napkins to give a special touch to your display.*

- *Try using your dining room chairs for your buffet display instead of your table.*

- *A nice rose tea in a pitcher with small teacups is a great addition to this snacktivity.*

chickpea waffles

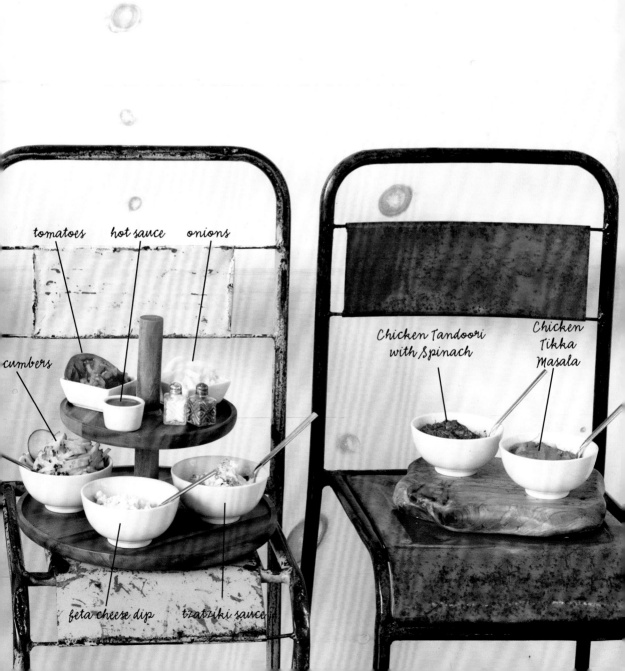

tomatoes   hot sauce   onions

cumbers

Chicken Tandoori
with Spinach

Chicken
Tikka
Masala

feta cheese dip   tzatziki sauce

SAVORY VODKA BAR

The night before your cocktail party, you can flavor your vodka to make all sorts of surprise cocktail concoctions. Here's a list of some fun things to flavor your vodka with: bacon, jalapeños, mushrooms, onions, rosemary, cucumber, Oreos, marshmallows, even doughnuts. There are zillions of great vodka-infusion recipes you can find online. So choose two or three and display.

- *Fill drink dispensers with a red, yellow, and green pepper medly, basil, and jalapeño-infused vodkas (as shown).*

- *Fill glass pitchers with juice mixers, so your guests can mix and match the ingredients to come up with that one great or horrible cocktail. Grapefruit, tomato, and lemonade are the mixers I choose, but you can go nuts with all sorts of flavor combinations.*

- *Set out shakers and a bowl of ice.*

- *Straws would be good for this one.*

- *Use mason jars for glasses, just in case you need a little extra shake.*

- *For a real surprise, be drunk by the time your guests arrive.* Kidding . . . sort of.

If you are really throwing a traditional surprise party, hide one last guest (maybe the one who traveled the farthest), and shortly after the big reveal, have this guest walk in, all casual. I love a surprise after a surprise.

I'm also a big fan of the confetti bomb, and there is never a more appropriate occasion to set one off than a surprise party. If thirty people yelling "SURPRISE!" at the birthday boy or girl doesn't scare the crap out of them, then launching a bunch of confetti bombs (available at party stores or online) will certainly do the trick.

PARTY FOULS

How to remove:

CANDLE WAX

Fill a plastic bag with ice and place on the area with the candle wax until the wax is hard, then use a knife (preferably a butter knife) to remove.

CHOCOLATE CAKE

Soak a kitchen towel with hot water and squeeze out excess water, add one squirt of liquid dish soap to the towel and carefully rub the stain until it is removed.

CONFETTI

Leave it . . . It's pretty or your boyfriend, the DustBuster, should do the trick.

RED WINE

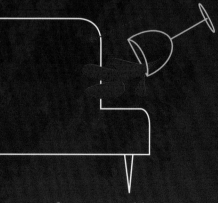

Get a new couch!

☑ Mop
☑ Broom
☑ Vacuum for confetti
☑ Next time hire caterer
☑ Throw out couch
☑ Move

THE COCKTAIL PARTY

Cleaning Supply List to Cover All Party Surprises

Have the vacuum cleaner and several clean, empty vacuum bags handy to pick up all that damn confetti that is now spread out all over your floor. Or move.

How about a post-party cleaning supply checklist, to make sure you're prepared for surprise messes?

Garbage bags (I always keep an extra at the bottom of the bin for quick replacement), furniture or carpet stain remover, paper towels, and floor cleaner. Best advice: Clean as you go. I do not start my party with dirty dishes in my sink or an unnecessary mess on my kitchen counter. This makes for a much more organized party and gives you less to worry about once your guests are gone.

But don't start cleaning up while the party is still going on, that's just bad form.

SURPRISE POOL PARTY . . . SORT OF

Our first house in Woodstock, New York, was literally 850 square feet. Having weekend guests over (which was every weekend—I live for this sort of thing!) challenged me to reinvent entertaining norms. This was a lot easier in the summer, when I had the use of my backyard, which gave me a whole new world of opportunities in which to entertain with a twist. When I'd exhausted every tree-shaded patch of grass, I went to a place that was, well, maybe a bit extreme.

For years, I had been talking about having a dinner party at the bottom of our swimming pool.

"Like underwater?" Ryan asked me the first time I broached this bizarre idea with him.

"No, like *empty*, no water. One beautifully set table with food, music, and friends."

"Sure, Mary," Ryan said.

Same "Sure, Mary" I get about five times a month, when I run my brilliant ideas by him . . . like:

"We should turn our basement into a disco (like in *The Jerk*)."

Or . . .

"What is an alpaca? Do we have enough room in our backyard for one?"

But, a few summers ago, Ryan actually gave in to one of my ideas and we put together a last-minute dinner party in the bottom of our empty swimming pool. We invited two friends who we were sure wouldn't ask too many questions.

"Hey, wanna have dinner at the bottom of our empty swimming pool?"

"Sure, what time?"

Did I mention how much I love our Woodstock friends?

So I quickly went to work.

"You're *crazy*," Ryan said as he carried our breakfast table into the pool. But when I get "you're crazy" with a smile or a laugh from him, I know I'm not in too much trouble and he is having fun too.

Soooo . . . table is set, wine is poured, music is blasting from our portable sound system, and just as I am about to go up and get the dinner from our kitchen (cioppino, by the way) and bring it down to the pool . . .

The pool guys show up, a day early, with our water delivery! *Foiled!* Our dinner party was over before it began.

I pleaded with the nice gents to come back another time, even tried to bribe them with some vino, but no luck. My pool party dream was ruined.

Finally, I asked if they would mind if we took a few pictures before they turned on the hose and washed away my vision (okay . . . a little melodramatic, I know).

One of them looked at me, smiling, and said, "No problem. In twenty-eight years of working with swimming pools, ma'am, I've never seen anything like this."

Mission accomplished.

This idea, of course, is a bit extreme, and perhaps way out of your wheelhouse. So, instead of draining your swimming pool or bathtub (hmmm), use the ideas in this chapter to have some fun and serve up surprises in menu, guests, and location.

Oh, and an alpaca is a type of camel. (I'm still working on this, by the way.) ⇉🐝⇇

CHAPTER 7

Cinco de Mayo

EAT

Spicy Pigs

Black Bean Cakes with Guacamole, Salsa, and Fried Onions

Sweet Quesadilla Bites

DRINK

Grapefruit-Jalapeño Margarita

Skinny "Fat Girl" Margarita

PLAY

Taco Bar

Tequila Bar

RECOVER

Seis de Mayo Hangover Kit

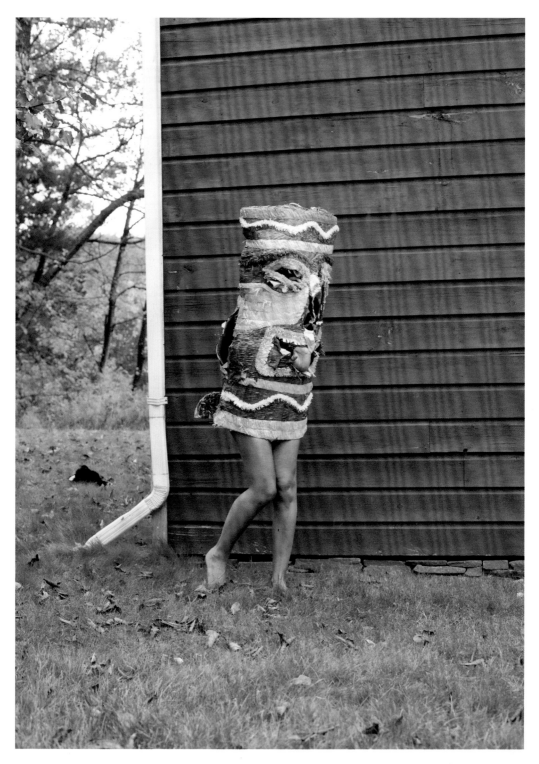

Here is a short quiz:

1) What's your drink? Are you a dirty-martini girl or a G&T guy? Are you the one glass of champagne on a special occasion kinda lady or the "I don't need an occasion to drink an entire bottle of champagne (by myself)" kinda dame?

2) Do you need an excuse or change of locale that requires airline travel to imbibe? Like, on vacation with a pretty drink umbrella? Or as a reward after a long day on the slopes?

3) Are you like me? A person who likes to drink with four A's (clearly not to be confused with AA)—anything, anywhere, anytime, with anyone.

If you answered yes to that last question, then you, like me, probably thank your lucky stars that there is an actual calendar event that says, "Go ahead and drink tequila and lots of it, and *even better* if you do it while wearing a sombrero and eating nachos!"

So I have decided to devote an entire chapter to the art of Cinco de Mayo entertaining. Give the day the respect it deserves, I say, and to this I raise my glass. . . .

I'll even let you in on a few tips for how to deal with the Seis de Mayo hangover (hopefully I'll spare you the embarrassment of waking up with a piñata over your head . . . not proud, ladies and gentlemen . . . not proud).

Love,
Mary

SPICY PIGS

1 egg yolk

3 tablespoons water

All-purpose flour for work surface

1 17-ounce package puff pastry sheets, thawed

1 16-ounce package chorizo sausages, ends trimmed

Deli mustard (in a squeeze bottle if possible)

Sesame seeds (optional)

Guacamole, store bought

YIELD: 24 PIECES
PREP TIME: 45 MINUTES • COOK TIME: 20 MINUTES

1. Preheat the oven to 375°F. Line a baking sheet with parchment paper.

2. Mix the egg yolk with the water to make an egg wash.

3. Lightly dust a work surface with flour, and place 1 sheet of the puff pastry on it.

4. Working with a long side of the sheet closest to you, place a chorizo at the edge across the pastry sheet. Line another chorizo next to the first so they are "kissing." This should fit end to end on the pastry sheet; if the chorizo extends past the sheet, cut a piece off to make it even and begin the next roll with the cut piece.

5. Squeeze mustard on the pastry along the chorizo.

6. Carefully roll the pastry dough over the sausage until it meets the mustard line. Brush the pastry dough with the egg wash end to end about ½ inch wide. Continue to roll the dough over the egg-washed dough to create an overlap. With a small knife, cut off the excess dough. Repeat until you have used all the sausage.

7. Carefully place the chorizo rolls on the baking sheet lined with parchment paper and freeze for about 30 minutes to stiffen.

8. Remove the chorizo rolls from the freezer onto a cutting board. Cut 1-inch slices and arrange the pieces spaced out on the baking sheet. The seam side should be facing down. If the pastry starts to get soft while cutting, place the chorizo rolls back in the freezer for 10 minutes before baking for uniform cooking.

9. Brush the tops with the egg wash. For extra flavor, sprinkle with sesame seeds.

10. Bake until golden brown, about 20 minutes.

11. Serve on a decorative platter or pass as a small bite with the guacamole.

BLACK BEAN CAKES WITH GUACAMOLE, SALSA, AND FRIED ONIONS

Hands down the most creative client that I work with is clothing designer Stella McCartney and her parties are always a hit. She is vegan, so we are always looking for exciting new ways to impress her guests with comforty favorites. This recipe can also be made into little sliders by adding a mini bun.

YIELD: 24 BEAN CAKES
PREP TIME: 20 MINUTES • COOK TIME: 15 TO 18 MINUTES

1. In a food processor, puree the beans, salsa, cumin, and coriander until halfway smooth. You should still see pieces of the beans.

2. Scrape the bean mixture into a medium bowl. Add the panko, cilantro, scallions, salt, and hot sauce. Taste and adjust the seasonings to your liking.

3. Line a baking sheet with parchment paper. Use a mini 25mm ice cream scoop to divide the mixture into equal portions. With your hands, form small patties. Place on the prepared baking sheet and store in the refrigerator for at least 30 minutes or overnight.

4. In a large frying pan, heat the olive oil for 8 to 10 minutes, then fry each patty for 5 to 8 minutes.

5. Remove the cakes with a draining spoon and drain on paper towels. Dot the top of each patty with guacamole, salsa, and curlicues of fried onions before serving.

6. Serve on a decorative platter or pass as a small bite.

1 15-ounce can black beans, rinsed and drained

½ cup salsa, mild or medium (plus extra for serving)

1 teaspoon ground cumin

1 teaspoon ground coriander

¼ cup panko (Japanese bread crumbs)

½ cup finely chopped fresh cilantro

½ cup thin-sliced scallions

1 teaspoons salt

½ teaspoon sriracha or other hot sauce

½ cup olive oil

½ cup guacamole (store bought or your favorite homemade recipe)

1 2.8-ounce can French's Fried Onions

Party Prep Playlist

"Tequila" (The Champs), "You and Tequila" (Kenney Chesney and Grace Potter), "Hey Nineteen" (Steely Dan), "Cheap Tequila" (Johnny Winter), "La Bamba" (Richie Valens), "Señorita" (Justin Timberlake), "Oh, What a Night" (Frankie Valli), "Sweet Caroline" (Neil Diamond), "Closing Time" (Semisonic), "Drunk in Love" (Beyoncé), "Drinking Tequila" (Jim Reeves), "Ring of Fire" (Johnny Cash)

SWEET QUESADILLA BITES

6 small (6-inch) flour tortillas

2 tablespoons unsalted butter

8 ounces (8 squares) dark chocolate, chopped

12 ounces Brie cheese, rind removed and sliced thin

This sweet variation on the usual savory quesadilla is so easy to make and a definite party wow. These can all be prepared prior to your guests arriving and then just reheated and served at dessert time.

YIELD: 24 QUESADILLA BITES
PREP TIME: 10 MINUTES • COOK TIME: 15 TO 18 MINUTES

1. Heat a large nonstick skillet over medium heat. Spread one side of each tortilla with the butter and place, butter side down, in the pan. Top with the chocolate and a layer of Brie. Place another buttered tortilla on top with the butter side up.

2. Cook until the chocolate and cheese start to melt, about 3 minutes. Carefully flip over and cook on the other side until evenly browned. Remove from the heat and rest the quesadilla on a cutting board for 3 minutes. Repeat for the other quesadillas.

3. Cut each into 8 small triangles.

4. Serve on a decorative platter or pass as a small bite.

GRAPEFRUIT-JALAPEÑO MARGARITA

This drink is so refreshing, with just the perfect amount of kick! The mixture of the light pink and the green looks so pretty, the drink dispenser can be all the décor you need.

YIELD: 12 SERVINGS

- 2 quarts pink grapefruit juice
- 18 ounces tequila (preferably Patrón)

   Jalapeño peppers, sliced thin (amount will depend on how much "heat" you like)

- ¾ cup agave syrup

Combine the ingredients in a drink dispenser of your choice. Serve over ice in rocks glasses. Garnish with additional jalapeño slices.

SKINNY "FAT GIRL" MARGARITA

- 1 litre bottle tequila (Casamigos is my *favorite*, and not just because George Clooney's name is on the bottle . . . it's *really* good.)
- 2 cups grapefruit juice

Combine and serve over ice without salt.

TACO BAR

A taco bar is one of the easiest ways to make it look like you've made a huge effort, when in reality all you did was dump things into bowls and arrange them neatly. All the food shown in this photo comes from Chipotle To-Go.

- *The only items that need to be heated or cooked are the proteins/meats you choose and the tortillas. All the other items can be store-bought and displayed.*

- *You can wrap your tortillas in a dish towel and heat in the oven on low heat for 20 minutes before you are ready to serve.*

- *Since this is a heat-and-serve station, use the extra time to find a unique or unexpected surface to serve from.*

- *A festive runner is a great way to say* Olé! *and will also catch spills.*

TEQUILA BAR (OR IN THIS CASE, TREE)

This is a great opportunity for a tequila tasting.

- *Display a few bottles of your favorite tequilas either on a table or hanging from a tree near your buffet as shown.*

- *In a tub filled with crushed ice, place decanters with fresh juices (grapefruit and lime) or packaged mixers.*

- *Sea salt, pink Himalayan salt, sliced limes, and grapefruit slices are great garnishes. Chasing a tequila shot with a grapefruit slice is very yummy.*

- *Set out a blender, shaker, and bowl of ice, so guests can choose which way they want their drink.*

- *Set out a variety of glasses, such as tasting glasses, martini glasses, and hurricane glasses.*

- *Straws are good for this type of bar.*

La Aspirina

Mentas

ALKA SELTZER

Seis de Mayo Hangover Kit

A Seis de Mayo recovery kit will help ensure that your guests will be a little less angry with you the next day (since you're the one who convinced them to play a drinking game called Cinco de Bingo). This recovery kit includes: aspirin, Alka-Seltzer, mints, and a hair tie (gross, but just in case).

YOU KNOW WHO ELSE LIKES MARGARITAS? OPRAH.

The email every caterer dreams of receiving . . .

....

Are you available to cater the after party for the opening night of *The Color Purple* on Broadway? It will be for approximately 200 guests and Oprah is scheduled to attend.

....

What? Oprah?! *My Oprah?* Sure enough, it was right there on my screen. I was finally going to have my Big O moment!

I had just two days to prepare, but really, I had been preparing for this moment my whole life. Well, really since I saw Rachael Ray whip up a batch of margaritas on Oprah's show and high-five each other while they took big long sips. That day, I began to dream of my high-five.

I knew that no matter how important this opportunity was for my then-growing catering business, this to me was a much bigger-picture moment. You see, I saw this as a one-way ticket to Oprah Land. Where the pancakes were thick and the butter always perfectly melted, where hot chocolate flowed in rivers and grilled cheese fell from the sky. Where Oprah and I would sit by the fire and she would ask me to tell her "that story" just one more time while she laughed with enjoyment at my devilishly witty humor.

In Oprah Land we would ride around in hovercrafts that existed exclusively for Oprah's use and we would land on Oprah Island, where sherpas would bring us cashmere blankets and lather our faces with the best moisturizers on the planet. When they were done, a leprechaun would wrap us up in Spanx and tuck us into beds made of clouds that Oprah had specially flown in from Nepal.

Oprah Land was finally within my reach.

By the time the party rolled around, I had already notified my husband and my family of my impending discovery and thanked them for the years of encouragement and support they had provided that brought me to this moment. It was probably just how Joe Pesci's character in *Goodfellas* felt on that car ride from the diner to that basement in Queens . . . I was going to be "made."

THE BIG DAY I arrived four hours early. I had to make sure that everything was *perfect*. I arranged the trays in the order I wanted the food to be presented, a perfect blend of fun and fine cuisine with touches of culinary humor, including the mini pulled pork truffle grilled cheese that I knew my Oprah would love paired with a signature margarita that I created just for her, The Color Purple, which was a purple margarita dusted with crystallized violet.

When the waiters arrived, I asked that we all gather in the kitchen for a special meeting. I asked them to hand over their cell phones, so as not to compromise The Big O's security. I stressed the utmost significance of this event and even uttered the now-embarrassing statement "This is the single most important night of my entire career." I instructed the staff that champagne must flow steadily; food should be visible in every corner; and as soon as Ms. Winfrey arrives, please make sure that I am notified. I even assigned two VIP waiters to assist her all night with anything she might've needed: a drink, a cucumber towel, foot rub . . . *anything*!

It was an hour into the party when Rubin, one of our newer waiters and very conscientious, came running into the kitchen, overjoyed beyond belief to deliver this news: "Mary, she is here!"

I looked at my kitchen staff with pride, applied lip gloss, smoothed my skirt, instructed a waiter to follow me out with HER special tray, and began my journey into the party room. Before leaving the kitchen, I remember thinking, "I will probably never see these people again." I grabbed my sous chef, looked him in the eyes with extreme sincerity, and said, "Thank you, my friend, for your hard work and loyalty, it has been a fine pleasure working with you." I will never forget the confusion in his face, as he pondered, "Why the hell is she saying goodbye to me?"

The kitchen door swung open and out I walked, maneuvering through the crowded party with the skill of a ballet dancer, one step closer to *My Oprah,* one step closer to Oprah Land. Rubin took my hand and led me toward the library, where he said she was waiting. My heart began to beat faster, my palms growing sweaty.

AND THEN . . .

There she was . . . Star Jones, picking on a crudité display. Rubin smiled from ear to ear, giving me a huge thumbs-up while he stood behind her, beaming as if he'd managed to hand me the golden ticket. Dejected, I smiled at Star, turned on my heel, and headed back toward the kitchen, where I belonged. I later found out that Rubin had only been in the country for three months and had no idea who Oprah was.

Oprah never arrived. At the end of my night, it was just me, left with a tray filled with four of "my Oprah's" watered-down purple margaritas, so I did what every disappointed caterer would do . . . drank all of 'em.

CHAPTER 8

Garden Party

EAT
Mini Veggie Pot Pies

Mini Lentil Burgers

Peanut Butter–Carob Balls

Grilled Peaches with Ricotta and Honey

DRINK
Drunk Goddess

Beet It

PLAY
Edible Garden

Deviled Egg Dirt Bar

Gelato with Edible Flowers

RECOVER
How to Plant a Foolproof Fruit
and Veggie Garden

Springtime is the best time to entertain. I love it because my mom's birthday is actually on Earth Day, and she taught me everything I know when it comes to food and entertaining. It is also a great time to look outside for party inspiration, particularly from your garden or what's popping up at your local markets.

In 2005, we bought our first house in Woodstock, New York, and settled down in what we think of as paradise. Not only is it our retreat from All Things Crazy in our busy New York City lives, Woodstock has become the best testing ground for new food and entertaining concepts and it's where I am most inspired and get many of my creative ideas. I even have a Party Barn, which has become my party lab, where I can test out all my wild party ideas and recipes. You're all invited if you're ever passing through town. ☺

As it pertains to your parties, each spring is an opportunity for you to do some party spring-cleaning. It's a great time for you to dust off your platters, edit your "party closet," and make sure you are properly stocked for your upcoming spring-summer party season.

When thinking of spring entertaining, look around at all the plentiful flowers, fresh fruits and vegetables, and Grill Your Garden, or even better, Drink Your Garden . . . with a small side of fries, of course.

Love,
Mary

MINI VEGGIE POT PIES

YIELD: 24 MINI PIES
PREP TIME: 40 MINUTES • COOK TIME: 40 MINUTES

Basic Pie Dough

1½ cups all-purpose flour

¼ teaspoon salt

1 teaspoon granulated sugar

¼ pound (1 stick) cold unsalted butter, cut into small pieces

4 to 5 tablespoons ice water

Filling

2 tablespoons canola oil

1 cup total of your choice of spring vegetables (cut into ¼-inch dice). I like zucchini, red onion, summer corn, and English peas but you can choose any of your favorites.

1 teaspoon each salt and pepper

1 teaspoon chopped fresh rosemary

1 teaspoon chopped fresh thyme

1 cup vegetable broth

2 tablespoons salted butter

2 tablespoons all-purpose flour

Pastry

2 frozen puff pastry sheets, cut out to 1½-inch circles and kept chilled until ready to assemble

1 egg, lightly beaten

Salt, for garnish

1. For the Dough: Combine the flour, salt, and sugar in a large bowl and stir briefly until the mixture is aerated. Using a pastry blender or your fingers, cut the butter into the dry ingredients until you have pea-size pieces that are slightly yellow in color. Drizzle in 4 tablespoons of the ice water and mix just until the dough comes together. (Add the last tablespoon of ice water if necessary, but don't overwork the dough or it'll become tough.) Shape the dough into a flat disk, cover it in plastic wrap, and refrigerate for at least 30 minutes.

2. Preheat the oven to 375°F.

3. Roll out the dough to ⅛ inch thick and cut out 2½-inch circles. Place each in a 3-inch mini aluminum pie tin. Press the sides up against the walls of the tins. Fill the shells with pie weights or dried beans to prevent the dough from bubbling, and place the tins on a baking sheet.

4. Bake for about 20 minutes, until the pie shells are lightly colored. Allow to cool and remove the pie weights or beans, placing the tins back on the baking sheet.

5. For the Filling: In a large saucepan over medium heat, sauté the vegetables in the oil until soft. Season with the salt and pepper and let cool. Transfer to a large mixing bowl and add the rosemary and thyme. In the same saucepan add the butter and flour and stir making a paste. Add the vegetable broth and cook until thickened.

6. Fill the half-baked pie shells three-quarters full with the vegetable mix. Pour the thickened vegetable broth inside to the top.

7. Pull out the puff pastry circles and brush with egg wash. Place the egg-washed sides down over the shells and crimp the edges with a small fork to seal.

8. Brush the tops of the pot pies with egg wash and sprinkle with salt. Poke 3 small holes using a toothpick in the center of the tops to allow steam to escape. Bake for about 20 minutes, or until golden brown in color.

9. Serve on a decorative platter (close to party time to keep warm) or pass as a small bite.

MINI LENTIL BURGERS

A delicious veggie alternative to burgers and hot dogs.

1 cup beluga lentils

¼ cup canola oil

½ cup small-dice red onions

4 garlic cloves, chopped

½ teaspoon red pepper flakes

1 cup small-dice eggplant, skin on or off

1 cup sliced mushrooms

½ cup sunflower seeds

1 tablespoon tahini paste

1 tablespoon chopped fresh mint

2 teaspoons ground cumin

Kosher salt and black pepper

24 mini burger buns

YIELD: 24 BURGERS
PREP TIME: 30 MINUTES • COOK TIME: 12 TO 15 MINUTES

1. Wash and drain the lentils. In a medium saucepan, cover the lentils with 2 cups water and bring to a boil. Reduce to a simmer, cover, and cook 20 to 25 minutes, until tender. Remove the lid to cool and set aside. Drain if there is any water left.

2. In a medium sauté pan, heat the oil on medium heat. Add the onions and sauté for about 4 minutes, stirring occasionally until they are soft, then add the garlic and red pepper flakes cook for about 30 seconds. Add the eggplant and mushrooms, stir once, then let the ingredients cook for a few minutes before stirring again to allow for a little caramelization. Continue to cook the mixture until the eggplant and mushrooms have softened and any excess water released has evaporated. Set aside to cool slightly.

3. In a food processor, add the sunflower seeds and pulse until the seeds are coarsely chopped. Add the cooked lentils, the vegetable mixture, tahini, mint, and cumin. Pulse until the mixture is combined. It should be thick. Season with salt and pepper.

4. Transfer the mixture into a bowl and, using a small ice cream scoop, make evenly sized balls of the mixture. Form them into little patties and use the mini burger buns to adjust the portion size of the burgers to fit on each.

5. Preheat the oven to 350°F.

6. The burgers can be heated in the oven for 12 to 15 minutes until hot, or sautéed with a light dusting of flour and some oil in a pan on medium heat to create a golden crust on the outside. Serve hot on the burger buns.

PEANUT BUTTER–CAROB BALLS

My very healthy sister first turned me on to this delicious and super-easy recipe. You can also roll them in some sunflower seeds to give them that summer garden touch.

YIELD: 24 BALLS
PREP TIME: 15 MINUTES

1. Combine all the ingredients, except the coconut, in a bowl. Shape into small balls and roll in the coconut.

2. Chill until firm.

3. Serve on a decorative tray or platter.

1 cup natural peanut butter

½ cup carob powder

½ cup honey

¼ cup chopped dried cherries

¼ cup raw or toasted shredded coconut

Party Prep Playlist

"Back to the Garden" (Crosby, Stills, Nash & Young), *The Magic Garden* Song (Carole and Paula), "Garden Song" (Peter, Paul & Mary), "San Francisco" (Scott McKenzie), "Daydream Believer" (The Monkees), "Feeling Groovy" (Simon and Garfunkel), "I Love Paris" (Ella Fitzgerald), "Tiptoe Through the Tulips" (Tiny Tim), "Pure Imagination" (Willy Wonka Soundtrack), "Scarlet Begonias" (The Grateful Dead), "White Rabbit" (Grace Potter and the Nocturnals), "Happy" (Pharell Williams), "You Don't Bring Me Flowers" (Barbra Streisand)

GRILLED PEACHES WITH RICOTTA AND HONEY

1 baguette, cut into ¼-inch-thick slices

1½ tablespoons olive oil

3 peaches, ripe but not mushy

2 tablespoons canola oil

1 tablespoon granulated sugar

½ teaspoon salt

½ teaspoon ground cardamom

1 cup fresh ricotta, drained

Freshly ground pepper

⅓ cup honey

I love grilling a wide variety of fruits and vegetables. Kale, beets, sweet potatoes, pineapples, figs, you name it. How 'bout a Grill Your Garden Party?

YIELD: 24 SERVINGS
PREP TIME: 15 MINUTES • GRILL TIME: 5 MINUTES

1. Preheat the oven to 375°F.

2. In a bowl, toss the sliced baguette with the olive oil to lightly coat the bread. Place on a baking sheet in a single layer and bake until golden brown, about 6 minutes. Remove and set aside to cool.

3. Preheat a hot grill or cast-iron grill pan. Split the peaches down the center, starting from the top, and remove the pits from both sides. Lay the peach halves flesh side down and cut into 4 even wedges per half and place in a bowl. Add the canola oil, sugar, salt, and cardamom, and gently toss to coat.

4. Grill the peach wedges for about 2 minutes, then turn them each clockwise about 45 degrees to create grill marks. Cook for another minute. Using a tong and a fork, carefully flip each one over and grill for 2 more minutes. Remove from the grill to cool slightly.

5. When ready to serve, spread an even layer of ricotta on top of each slice of crostini and sprinkle with freshly ground pepper.

6. In a small bowl, microwave the honey for 20 seconds to warm and liquefy it.

7. Lay the peach slices on the crostini. Using a spoon, dip into the warm honey and drizzle some over each peach.

8. Serve as described or with toothpicks for easier pick up.

DRUNK GODDESS

I'll probably go to some sort of health nut jail for these two, but hey—it's a party book! What's wrong with being healthy and naughty at the same time?

YIELD: 12 SERVINGS

- 6 handfuls kale leaves
- 6 handfuls spinach leaves
- 6 whole cucumbers
- 3 lemons, halved
- 1 tablespoon cayenne pepper
- 1 bottle of vodka

Combine all ingredients in a juicer or blender and blend well until combined. Pour into a rocks glass. Serve over ice.

BEET IT

YIELD: 12 SERVINGS

- 1½ quarts beet juice
- ½ bottle of vodka

Combine the juice and vodka in a drink dispenser of your choice. Mix well. Serve in wineglasses.

HOW ABOUT AN INFUSED-WATER BAR?
Set out glass drink dispensers with different fruits and veggies (cucumber, grapefruit, oranges, lemons, basil, jalapeños) infused into the water. Serve with glass mason jars and biodegradable straws.
Or an . . .

HERB GARDEN BAR
Instead of flowers on your bar, how about some potted herbs like basil, mint, and thyme? They look pretty, and guests can put a little "spring" into their glass.

EDIBLE GARDEN

Pretend the quinoa is potting soil. Slice up a
bunch of different veggies and display them
in a bed of quinoa. Guests can pile up on
healthy foods and it looks great, too. That's
how easy this is!

- *Fill planting/garden pots and trays with
  cooked quinoa; add carrots, radishes,
  tomatoes, blanched asparagus, zucchini,
  and yellow squash.*

- *Serve with Annie's ranch or goddess
  dressing, or any of your favorite homemade
  dips.*

- *Terra-cotta pots are also great vessels to
  display breadsticks, crudites, dips, etc.*

- *A wet paper towel placed over the veggies
  keeps them crisp until your party guests
  arrive.*

DEVILED EGG DIRT BAR

Everyone loves deviled eggs at a picnic. This is a great way to display them with a little garden twist.

- *Display 2 dozen deviled eggs (I love Ina Garten's recipe).*

- *In small metal or ceramic pails (you can find these at any craft store), put your "dirts": cayenne pepper, mustard powder, caper powder, tarragon, chives, sea salt, and pepper. You can find small shovels at your craft store, too.*

- *Set out with small plates and napkins and watch your guests devil up their eggs!*

GELATO WITH EDIBLE FLOWERS

Serve your favorite fresh fruit gelato with a bowlful of flowers (instead of sprinkles). Edible flowers can be found at any gourmet store. Some flowers that are safe to eat: calendula, carnation, chamomile, chicory, dandelion, gladiola, impatiens, lilac, violet, pansy, sage, and sunflower.

How to Plant a Foolproof Fruit and Veggie Garden

Watching something grow that you planted and then harvesting it is highly therapeutic. Don't have the green thumb but dream of growing a garden? Pick your favorite fruit or veggie that's easy to grow. Start with one . . . I promise, after you prove to yourself that you can keep that one fruit or veggie alive, you'll be hooked and inspired to plant more.

You can also have a planting party. Serve lots of good food and drink and have your friends help you plant . . . then you can say, "Those are Nancy's tomatoes or Nanette's kale."

BACK TO THE GARDEN

I was told early on by my parents that there are mountain people and there are beach people, "and you, Mary, are a beach person." So, I believed them, my family, as we had deep ties to the beachfront community of Montauk, where my grandmother Lucille had been a business pioneer, opening one of the first hotels there. But really, deep down inside, I yearned to do what all my other friends were doing: packing their trunks and heading off to sleepaway camp.

Don't get me wrong; I loved that we spent every summer going to the beach. But around springtime, I would begin to dread the end of the school year, because this was a time when my schoolmates grew increasingly more excited to head off to a land that was completely foreign to me . . . the mountains.

I already felt like an outsider, being one of the only girls from Great Neck who wasn't Jewish, though throughout the school year, I held my own. But when springtime camp excitement began, it was obvious that I was not one of the girls.

I remember sitting with my best friend, Lauren Balkin, in her bedroom as her mother packed her camp trunk for the summer: T-shirts, bug spray, paper for letter writing, stamps. While my friends were off to spend their summers drinking bug juice, learning how to give hand jobs, and racing in color wars, I was headed to Montauk to read books, check in guests at my grandmother's hotel, and play cards with my Grandpa Charlie. . . . There would be no encounters with some cute boy from Syosset named Seth who knew how to unhook my bra with just one hand.

Just once I wanted to come back from a summer and tell stories to my friends like they would tell to me. I yearned to sneak out after lights-out and skinny-dip with the boys from the camp across the lake. I wanted to go to sleepaway camp so badly that at twelve years old, I called Camp Towanda with a napkin over the phone receiver, pretended to be my mother, and requested that the camp owners, Sam and Lynn Nordan, travel from Honesdale, Pennsylvania, to Great Neck, Long Island, to talk to our family about their camp. Back then, this was common practice— camp representatives made home visits, schmoozed with the parents, gave the kids free T-shirts, and usually left with a check.

I will never forget sitting at the dinner table when the doorbell rang that night. "Are you expecting anyone, Robbie?" my mother asked my father as he looked at her, puzzled, and headed for the door. Sure enough, Sam and Lynn Nordan were at our door, equipped with Camp Towanda hats, T-shirts, and a pull-down screen and slide projector. My parents, confused but gracious, invited them into our home. "You are in big trouble," my mother whispered to me as she shot me a stern look and tried to offer the couple a plate of her spaghetti and meatballs. The slide show was tantalizing. I was drooling as I watched shot after shot of kids jumping off rocks into lakes, making arts and crafts, and playing foosball. When the presentation was over, my father looked at Sam Nordan with all sincerity and asked how I was going to get to church on Sunday. Sam was more than confused. "I'm sure we can work something out, but . . . Camp Towanda is a predominantly Jewish camp."

Sam and Lynn quickly rolled up their

screen, loaded it back into their car, took back the Towanda hat that sat atop my head, and that was that. I couldn't stop crying that night as my mother tucked me in, imparting her great wisdom about summer camp and the drunken indifferent mothers who sent their kids there. I remember praying so hard that night, "Dear God, please make my mother an alcoholic so that I can go to camp."

Sadly, to this day, I have never even so much as seen a real camp, and my mother? She's yet to have a sip of alcohol (not since her honeymoon, when, after one rum punch, she couldn't feel her legs . . . if I had a dime for every time I heard that story . . .), but I did *finally* make it to the Catskill Mountains and now proudly call the town of Woodstock home, where I entertain as if it is my adult sleepaway camp. Now instead of springtime bringing me dread and sadness, it has become my favorite time to entertain. And you want to know the best part? Ryan knows how to unhook my bra with just one hand.

CHAPTER 9

Baby Shower

EAT

Burrata Balsamic Crostini

ALT Club with Roasted Garlic Mayonnaise

Rocky Road Fudge Bars

Pink and Blue Rock Candy Brownies

DRINK

Lavender Lemonade

Mint Julep Iced Tea

Frozen Flower Cubes

PLAY

Ice Cream & Pickle Bar

Tea Sandwich Display

RECOVER

How 'Bout Mama? Giving Tree Takeaway for
Baby Mamas

I've always been drawn to Southern hospitality, but when I heard about the tradition of a sip 'n' see, I was hooked. This baby shower—inspired gathering is essentially a cocktail party that happens after the baby is already home and being marinated in lots of love. It is a great excuse for a (co-ed) party where your guests can meet the baby while drinking lots of mint juleps. It can take place on a Friday or Saturday night (when people actually like going out) as opposed to that dreaded 2 p.m. Saturday or Sunday traditional baby-shower time.

This is the perfect fête for any type of new-addition celebration—families-in-waiting, the surrogates, the adoption advocates, the single-but-choosing-to-be-parents, and all the rest of the wonderful and loving straight and gay people out there, just hopin' and prayin' and waitin' to open their hearts and homes to the baby of their dreams.

What I do know is that where there is a will, there is a way, and I would be more than honored to plan *all* of your sip 'n' sees when your journey is complete.

(And, while you're waiting, the Cinco de Mayo chapter may be a helpful diversion.)

Love,
Mary

BURRATA BALSAMIC CROSTINI

1 to 2 loaves sturdy Italian bread or baguette

½ pint grape or cherry tomatoes

6 leaves fresh basil, thinly sliced right before serving

1 teaspoon dried oregano (Sicilian, if possible)

¼ cup extra-virgin olive oil

Salt and pepper

1 8-ounce ball fresh burrata

1 tablespoon balsamic vinegar

Following our "Almost Homemade" formula, I recommend making these bites in addition to some store-ordered pre-made tea sandwiches, if you are looking to save time. You can also top this crostini with pancetta for a little extraspecial touch.

YIELD: 24 CROSTINI
PREP TIME: 15 MINUTES

1. Preheat the oven to 350°F.

2. Cut the bread into 24 slices approximately ½ inch thick. Arrange the slices on a baking sheet and toast in the oven until golden, about 6 minutes, turning once to toast both sides.

3. Slice about 10 tomatoes vertically in ¼-inch slices and place them in a small bowl.

4. Add the sliced basil to the tomatoes with the oregano and olive oil. Season with salt and pepper to taste.

5. Shingle 2 or 3 slices of the tomatoes across the tops of the crostini.

6. Slice the burrata down the center to expose the cheese curd and spoon out small portions of the liquid cheese onto the tomatoes. Dice the solid outer portion of the burrata, and lightly press some chunks onto each crostini.

7. Sprinkle the tops with salt and pepper. Drizzle the balsamic vinegar over the crostini and an additional drop of extra-virgin olive oil before serving.

wigwam

ALT CLUB

6 slices sourdough bread, cut about ⅓ inch thick and crusts trimmed

½ pint grape or cherry tomatoes

1 bunch (about 2 cups) watercress or baby arugula leaves

½ avocado, ripe but not mushy

¼ cup Roasted Garlic Mayonnaise (recipe follows), plus additional for garnish

Salt and pepper

YIELD: 24 SANDWICH BITES
PREP TIME: 15 MINUTES

1. Preheat the oven to 350°F.

2. Cut each slice of bread into quarters. Place the slices on a baking sheet and bake for about 8 minutes, or until lightly golden brown.

3. Slice the tomatoes into ¼-inch circles and set aside.

4. Remove the watercress or arugula leaves from the stems and discard the stems.

5. When ready to assemble, cut the avocado in half and remove the pit and skin. Cut the avocado into ¼-inch-thick slices and then into even-size shapes, such as triangles, for a uniform look.

6. Squeeze a dollop of Roasted Garlic Mayonnaise on top of the square toast points. Place 2 slices of the tomatoes on top, followed by watercress leaves, then a slice of avocado. Season with salt and pepper and garnish with a dot of mayonnaise.

ROASTED GARLIC MAYONNAISE

5 cloves peeled garlic

2 tablespoons olive oil

1 cup mayonnaise

1 teaspoon salt, or to taste

½ teaspoon black pepper

Zest and juice of ½ lemon

YIELD: 1¼ CUPS
PREP TIME: 15 MINUTES • COOK TIME: 25 MINUTES

1. Preheat the oven to 350°F.

2. Place a sheet of foil about 6 inches square on a work surface. Place the garlic cloves in the center and spoon the oil on top. Bring the foil ends up and over to the center to create a purse and fold the foil together to seal the garlic and oil inside.

3. Put the purse on a small tray or sauté pan and bake for about 25 minutes, or until soft. Remove from the oven and let cool.

4. In a food processor, add the oil and garlic, the mayonnaise, salt, pepper, lemon juice, and zest and puree to combine. Adjust seasoning to taste.

5. Place in an airtight container and store in the refrigerator up to a week. You have more than needed for the ALT Club recipe, so spread the garlicky love!

ROCKY ROAD FUDGE BARS

YIELD: 24 BARS
PREP TIME: 10 MINUTES • COOK TIME: 15 MINUTES
COOL TIME: 3 TO 4 HOURS

1. In a medium-size saucepan over medium-high heat mix the sugar and milk together. Bring to a boil and cook for exactly 8 minutes (this registers as the soft ball stage on a candy thermometer, if you are using one).

2. Remove the mixture from the heat and add the butter and marshmallow creme and stir until smooth. Add the chocolate and mix until melted (if the mixture looks "broken," beat with a wooden spoon or the paddle attachment of a stand mixer until smooth and fluid). Add in the marshmallows, peanuts, vanilla, and salt and mix until incorporated.

3. Pour into a greased 9-inch square pan. Cool completely in the refrigerator before removing from the pan and cutting into squares.

1¾ cups sugar

½ 6-ounce can evaporated milk

¼ pound (1 stick) unsalted butter

½ 7-oz jar marshmallow creme

2½ cups chopped bittersweet chocolate or chips (65% dark)

½ bag large Jet-Puffed marshmallows, cut into quarters

¾ cup roasted peanuts

½ teaspoon vanilla extract

¼ teaspoon salt

PINK AND BLUE ROCK CANDY BROWNIES

1 18.3-ounce box Duncan Hines Chewy Fudge Brownie Mix

1 16 oz. tub of your favorite store-bought or homemade vanilla frosting. I like Duncan Hines Classic Vanilla for this recipe.

1 package each pink and blue Rock Candy

This recipe is really easy. One box of store-bought brownie mix will yield enough mini bites for your party. If you want to add a homemade touch to the store-bought, try subbing in coconut oil for the vegetable oil.

YIELD: 24 MINI BROWNIES
PREP TIME: 10 MINUTES • COOK TIME: 12 TO 15 MINUTES

1. Preheat the oven to 350°F.

2. Prepare the brownie mix according to the package directions.

3. Fill 2 mini muffin tins with the brownie mix. Bake according to the directions on the package.

4. Let cool about 20 minutes. With a knife or rubber spatula, top each brownie with vanilla frosting.

5. Sprinkle half of the mini brownies with pink Rock Candy and the remaining half with blue. Place on a platter and serve.

Party Prep Playlist

"Cuddly Toy" (The Monkees), "Blackbird" (The Beatles), "Baby Love" (The Supremes), "Can't Smile Without You" (Barry Manilow), "You Are My Sunshine" (Willie Nelson), "Annie's Song" (John Denver), "Beautiful Boy" (John Lennon), "Piece of Sky" (Barbra Streisand), "Imagine" (John Lennon), "Now and Forever" (Carole King), "Piece of My Heart" (Janis Joplin), "Flowers for Zoe" (Lenny Kravitz), "Mockingbird" (Carly Simon and James Taylor), "Mother and Child Reunion" (Paul Simon), "Soliloquy" (Frank Sinatra), "A Boy Named Sue" (Johnny Cash), "I'm a Believer" (The Monkees)

It's a baby shower, but it's at night . . . so permission granted to spike these daytime cocktails with some nighttime libations.

LAVENDER LEMONADE

YIELD: 8 TO 10 SERVINGS

- 1 gallon lemonade
- 6 food-grade lavender sprigs

Fill a drink dispenser with the lemonade and add the lavender sprigs. Serve in rocks glasses with ice.

MINT JULEP ICED TEA

YIELD: 10 TO 12 SERVINGS

- 1 gallon sweetened iced tea
- 8 ounces bourbon (I love Hudson bourbons)
- 1 cup fresh mint

1. Combine the tea and bourbon in a drink dispenser of your choice and mix well.

2. Serve in rocks glasses over ice.

3. Garnish with the mint.

FROZEN FLOWER CUBES

YIELD: APPROXIMATELY 36 ICE CUBES

Place edible flowers/berries of choice in empty ice cube trays. (See page 164 for choices.) Pour in cold water to fill the trays. Place in the freezer overnight.

Make sure you have a wine for drinkers (the ones who will drink until they need a diaper) and nonalcoholic options for the guest of honor, designated drivers, and anyone else who doesn't feel like imbibing. Fresh berries in sparkling water is a simple and elegant way to do the trick.

ICE CREAM & PICKLE BAR

Fill a tub or bucket with ice and place assorted pints of ice cream in
it. Place ice cream scoops and a bowl of hot water in front to clean
the scoops.

- *Set out with bowls or coffee cups (as shown) and spoons.*

- *In decorative glass jars, place an assortment of pickles. You can
  actually buy a few types of jarred pickles, place them in warm
  water to remove the labels, then simply pop open the tops and serve.*

TEA SANDWICH DISPLAY

While tea sandwiches are traditionally served during the day . . . I say serve them at night too! Remember, we are not following traditional rules.

- *Set plates and tiered stands at various heights.*

- *Make sure you have a variety of tea sandwiches—several different fillings as well as different types of bread. (I like one veggie, two meats, and one egg salad.)*

- *All sandwiches should be approximately bite-size, and you should have two types of sandwiches per person.*

- *Add one type of biscuit or scone (I love a Cheddar and ham biscuit) to put a little diversity in the look.*

- *Small plates and linen cocktail napkins are the only things needed for this tea sandwich display.*

You can also use gifts as the décor. Children's books, blocks, bottles, and diapers can all be useful in the décor as well as useful swag for the new mom. Have your guests send ahead their unwrapped gifts (saves a tree or two), then use them as décor around the room. Make sure you have some large bags to fill and send Mom home with.

How 'Bout Mama? Giving Tree Takeaway
for Baby Mamas

Instead of buying a gift for the baby, gift the mom with a certificate for a massage or manicure or pedicure. Give her a little pre- or post-baby treat.

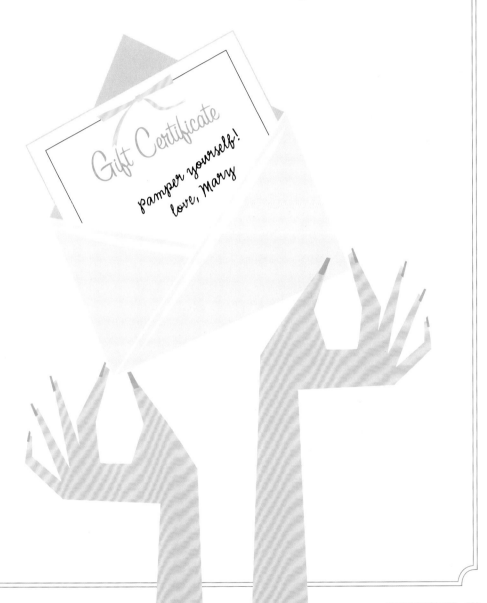

Gift Certificate

pamper yourself!
love, Mary

ELAINE'S

Some people come into your life as blessings, and others as lessons, and the rare and most treasured ones are both. For me, one of those was Elaine Kaufman.

I met Elaine nine years ago, when my cousin Brian asked Ryan and me to meet him uptown for dinner.

My only knowledge of Elaine's came from my childhood on Long Island, where one is expected to worship at the altar of Billy Joel. There's a lyric in his song "Big Shot" that goes: "They were all impressed with your Halston dress and the people that you knew at Elaine's." So, that's where we were heading, except that we didn't know anyone, and none of us was wearing Halston.

After a $17.00 cab ride, my anti-Billy/pro-Bruce (New Jersey) husband and I arrived at Elaine's.

I don't know if it was the glowing yellow sign flashing her name, the seventy-year-old bartender, the ex-cops drinking Maker's Mark, the smell of fried chicken cutlets waiting to be Parmesaned, or playwright Edward Albee sitting in the corner that got me, but one thing I knew for sure: I was in Elaine's house and I didn't want to leave.

We sat at a round table in the back and, as Ryan and Brian perused the menu, I could not stop looking around and taking it all in. I instantly knew that "things" happened here. Good, bad, wild, crazy . . . the energy was intense and enthralling.

"Does Elaine still come here?" I asked my cousin, who was a regular. "Yes, every night," he promised. "Just wait, you'll see her."

I ordered. I waited. Brian and I grew up with a grandmother who also went by one name, a woman who had the same powerful charisma, a woman who also made people wait.

The first course came. I was still waiting. Second course came. When the waiter came over and asked for our dessert order, I felt let down.

This wasn't the night; she wasn't here.

And then, as if a director yelled, "Action!" Elaine came in through the front door. Immediately, I saw people all around me who were pretending not to be fazed by her presence, pretending not to notice that a shift in energy had occurred in the room. "Be cool, don't look," I told myself.

But I couldn't help myself. Like the others, I was drawn to her, although she was really doing nothing at all. It seemed like the world was just rotating around her . . . but why?

"Mary, *stop* staring!" my husband begged, but I could not.

She made her way to HER table and sat, at first alone and then, occasionally, with others. I watched the whole restaurant try to plot how they would get to talk to her, or better yet—be invited to sit at HER table.

That first night, I was only able to get a smile in on our way out the door. It became my mission to get to know Elaine better. Obsession? You could say so. We began to go to Elaine's regularly. I ordered the same dish every time: tortellini with peas and prosciutto.

While all my peers wanted to go to the hottest spots downtown, Elaine's was the only place I wanted to be. Week by week, a smile, a wave, one night even a hello and then, one night (months later), our time had come. We were heading out and I glanced over to her to say goodbye. For the first time, she made direct eye contact with me.

"Sit down," she ordered.

It was as if she was handing me a million dollars and saying, "Take it and run, kid."

I sat down.

The questions began. "Who are you two?" Ryan began telling her our names, because I couldn't muster up the courage to speak. "Your husband says you work with celebrities?"

I just nodded yes. I was mute.

She began to speak: "Never give them anything for free. They'll ask you. You have to pay your bills and if you let one get away with it, they'll all think they can.

"If they can't pay you, make them promise to pay you when they can. They will have ups and downs like you . . . Don't forget that.

"Now get up. I'm leaving." She gestured to the waiter and he escorted her out.

I wanted to come back every week just to be in Elaine's presence, to learn from her, to watch her hold court. I dreamt that maybe one day, she would take me under her wing, tell me all her stories, teach me the ropes. I wanted her to be my "Tuesdays with Morrie."

As time passed, we got a little closer; we talked about bringing back her famous Oscar Night party. We were starting to make plans; she was beginning to like me. I'd tell her about a new client or cool party we did, and she would smile with approval. I think my excitement reminded her of her early days.

Perhaps my greatest lesson from Elaine would not be about food or table settings or celeb politics . . . Elaine shared with me a side that very few people got to see. So many stories were written about how tough she was, how she was crass, how she didn't like women and preferred the company of men. I'm not sure how many people saw the tender and caring side of Elaine, but I did and it felt like an amazing gift, a blessing, in fact . . . better and more special than the advice of one business-woman to another.

One night . . . late, maybe 1:30 or 2 a.m., I was telling her a tale about a new client with whom I was excited to be working, when mid-sentence she interrupted me, leaned in, and asked, "You have kids?"

I answered that we did not. I started to tell her our weary tales of unsuccessful baby making.

She looked me straight in the eye, paused, and then with a grandmother's sincerity, grabbed my hand and said, "*Have them.* That may end up being your best job."

Two weeks later, Elaine died. At eighty-one years old, Elaine left this world with no children or husband, but so many people felt the loss of her, loved her as their own.

I went to Elaine's by myself the night she died, on my way picking up a bouquet of white roses. It was mobbed, people waiting outside to go through those doors under that yellow sign. She would have loved the crowd. Inside, people shared stories, drinks, tears, and hugs.

Elaine taught me so much. But on the night she died, I realized that family comes in many forms, and that in my heart, she was a cherished member of mine.

CHAPTER 11

Weddings

EAT
Italian Wedding Mini Grilled Cheese

Black Truffle Gougères

White Chocolate S'mores

Champagne Macarons

DRINK
Blushing Bride aka Pink Gin & Tonic

Don't Stain My Dress aka White Sangria

PLAY
All-White Bar

Walking Food Bars

Old-Fashioned Champagne Tower

RECOVER
How to Avoid a Wedding Hangover

A Cocktail Party wedding!? You and Martha Stewart may say no, but I say YES, YES, YES!

September of this year, Ryan and I will celebrate our fifteenth wedding anniversary. I was twenty-four when I got married, a young bride by today's standards, and if I forget how young I was, I have the following items from my bridal registry to serve as a reminder: a glass frog, a fondue set, a popcorn machine, and a hot dog maker. To this day, I still do not own proper china, engraved dinner napkins, or fancy bath towels. Also, fifteen years later, I have yet to complete my wedding album.

People always assume, because I own a catering company that creates beautiful, over-the-top weddings, that I was one of those brides. And by "those brides," I'm referring to the ones who spend months trying on dresses, testing hairdos, tasting cakes, and picking flowers.

I am more of a no-fuss kind of gal, an antibride. And my quest in this chapter is to provide my fellow antibrides with all the tools that speak to them and actually make this the best day ever!

And, if I may circle back, while I still do not have the proper china or monogrammed towels fifteen years later, I still have one very important wedding gift—my husband! To me, that's much better than a completed wedding album or fancy registry.

Love,
Mary

P.S.: Okay, I will admit I would like one set of Frette linens before I die.

ITALIAN WEDDING MINI GRILLED CHEESE

2 tablespoons extra-virgin olive oil

1 to 2 cloves garlic, chopped

1 cup escarole, washed and chopped

Salt and pepper

2 cooked large-size leftover meatballs, chopped (store-bought are fine)

6 slices (¼ inch thick) good sturdy sandwich bread (I prefer *pain de mie*)

1 cup grated fontina cheese

¼ cup grated Parmesan or Romano cheese

2 tablespoons butter, melted

Nothing says I love you more than this cheesy, hearty, and comforty food in one bite.

YIELD: 24 PIECES
PREP TIME: 5 MINUTES • COOK TIME: 15 MINUTES

1. In a small sauté pan, heat the olive oil on medium-high heat for about 40 seconds. Add the garlic and stir for about 10 seconds, then add the escarole and sauté while stirring, about 3 minutes, until it is wilted and tender. Season with the salt and pepper. Set aside to cool.

2. Once the escarole is cooled down, wrap it in a clean, dry paper towel and gently wring it to squeeze out the excess water and oil. Place the escarole into a medium bowl.

3. Add the chopped meatballs, stir to combine, and adjust the seasonings.

4. Lay out 3 slices of bread on a clean work surface and spread the grated fontina on each slice. Place an even, thin layer of the escarole and meatball mixture on top of the cheese, followed by a generous sprinkle of grated Parmesan or Romano cheese. Add another thin layer of grated fontina on top and close the sandwiches with the remaining 3 slices of bread.

5. Brush the butter on the top of each sandwich.

6. Preheat a nonstick 10-inch sauté pan on low heat. Add the sandwiches one at a time, buttered side down, and cook for about 2 minutes, or until golden brown. Brush the top of each sandwich with butter while it cooks. Carefully flip the sandwich over and brown the other side.

7. Set the finished sandwiches on a cutting board and cut from corner to corner, creating 4 triangles. Cut each triangle in half again, giving you 8 mini triangles per sandwich.

8. Serve on a decorative platter or pass as a small bite.

BLACK TRUFFLE GOUGÈRES

These are a premium item, but hey, it's a wedding!

YIELD: 24 GOUGÈRES
PREP TIME: 15 MINUTES • COOK TIME: 12 TO 15 MINUTES

1. Preheat the oven to 325°F. Line a baking sheet with parchment paper.

2. In a saucepan, bring the milk, water, and butter to a boil. Remove from the heat and stir in the flour and salt. Place back on low heat and gently cook while stirring to dry out the mixture a little bit.

3. Place in a mixer with the paddle attachment. On low speed, incorporate the eggs one at a time. Finish with the Grana Padano, cayenne, truffle oil, and chives.

4. Using a pastry bag fitted with an open tip, pipe to the size of a quarter and bake for about 12 minutes, until golden brown.

5. Serve warm as an elegant passed hors d'oeuvre.

1 cup whole milk

1 cup water

½ pound (2 sticks) butter

1½ cups all-purpose flour

2 teaspoons salt

6 eggs

½ cup grated Grana Padano cheese

⅓ teaspoon cayenne pepper

½ black truffle oil (you can also use truffle salt as a cheaper option)

Chopped fresh chives

WHITE CHOCOLATE S'MORES

2 cups graham cracker crumbs (about one 14-ounce box)

½ pound (2 sticks) unsalted butter, softened

4 egg yolks, lightly beaten

¼ cup granulated sugar

¼ teaspoon salt

3 cups white chocolate chips

1 10½-ounce bag mini marshmallows

A dessert that matches the bride's dress, that tastes like chocolate but won't stain? Perfection!

YIELD: 24 S'MORES

PREP TIME: 60 MINUTES • COOK TIME: 20 MINUTES

1. In a food processor or large mixing bowl, combine the graham cracker crumbs, butter, egg yolks, sugar, and salt. Mix thoroughly.

2. Press the mixture evenly into a greased 12 x 17-inch baking pan and then put it into the refrigerator to chill for about 30 minutes.

3. Melt the white chocolate chips in a saucepan over low heat, stirring continuously.

4. Pour the melted chocolate over the graham cracker mixture and spread it out evenly with a spoon or rubber spatula.

5. Return the pan to the refrigerator for another 30 minutes, or until the chocolate hardens.

6. Cut out rounds using a ⅞-inch round cookie cutter or the smallest round cutter you can find (size of a quarter). Set aside.

7. Place about 30 mini marshmallows in a microwave-safe dish and heat on high for 15 seconds.

8. Spoon the melted marshmallow over 6 cookies at a time, continuing to melt small batches of marshmallows until all the cookies are covered.

9. Serve as part of a dessert buffet or pass on a decorative tray.

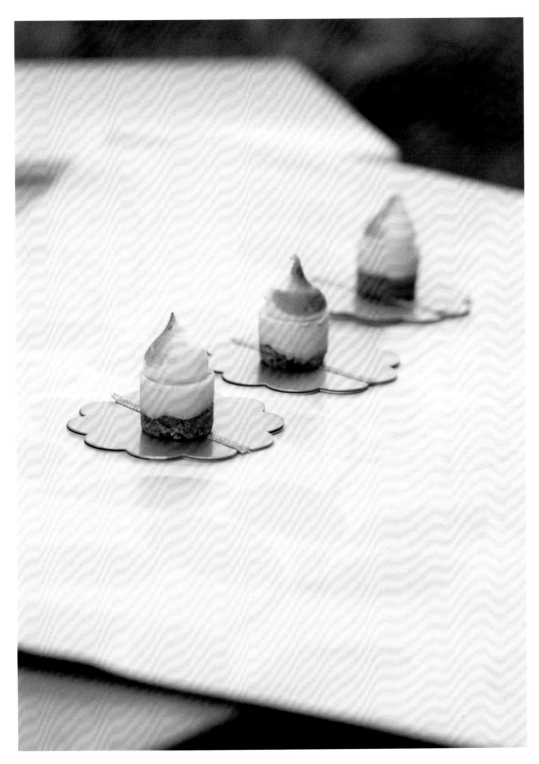

Ganache

- ⅔ cup roughly chopped 74% dark chocolate

- ⅓ cup roughly chopped milk chocolate

- 2 teaspoons Dutch cocoa powder

- ¼ cup plus 1 tablespoon praline/hazelnut paste

- ¼ teaspoon kosher salt

- ⅓ cup plus 2 tablespoons heavy cream

- ½ teaspoon vanilla extract

Champagne Gel

- 2 teaspoons apple pectin

- 1¼ cups granulated sugar

- 1 750ml bottle champagne

- ½ teaspoon citric acid powder

CHAMPAGNE MACARONS

These are really special and people go wild for them. Note that the hazelnut ganache filling and champagne gel used to edge the cookies need to be prepared a day ahead if possible. I know, I know . . . this recipe is a bit more work. You can cut one major corner here—you can substitute Nutella for the ganache, although I'll note that Nutella is a bit sweeter. So your call, but these are totally worth it, trust me!

YIELD: APPROXIMATELY 24 BITE-SIZE MACARONS

For the hazelnut ganache filling

PREP TIME: 10 MINUTES • COOK TIME: 5 MINUTES
COOL TIME: AT LEAST 2 TO 3 HOURS OR PREFERABLY
1 DAY AHEAD

1. For the Ganache: Place both chocolates, the cocoa powder, praline paste, and salt in a stainless-steel bowl. Set the bowl aside. In a medium saucepan, mix the cream and vanilla over medium heat, bringing it to a gentle boil.

2. Pour the cream mixture over the chocolate and wait 20 seconds, allowing the heat of the cream to melt the chocolate. Stir vigorously with a whisk until a blended, glossy ganache forms.

3. Cover the bowl with plastic wrap and allow it to cool in the refrigerator until it has reached a pipeable consistency.

For the champagne gel (this is enough for a double recipe of macarons)

PREP TIME: 5 MINUTES • COOK TIME: 30 TO 45 MINUTES
COOL TIME: OVERNIGHT

1. For the Champagne Gel: In a clean mixing bowl, mix the pectin and sugar and set aside.

2. In a tall-sided saucepan, bring the champagne to a boil. Add the sugar mixture and whisk to dissolve.

3. Bring the mixture back to a boil and reduce by two-thirds, until the mixture begins to get thick and syrupy. Be careful not to caramelize the mixture. Turn off the heat and pour the gel into another container to help reduce the temperature. Allow it to set for at least 12 hours in the refrigerator.

For the macarons

PREP TIME: 1 HOUR • BAKE TIME: 15 MINUTES
ASSEMBLY TIME: 15 MINUTES

Macarons

- 1 ½ cups blanched almond flour
- 1 ¼ cups confectioners' sugar
- Zest of ¼ lemon
- ⅛ teaspoon kosher salt
- 1 tablespoon plus 2 teaspoons water
- ½ cup superfine sugar
- 6 tablespoons plus 4 teaspoons pasteurized 100% egg whites, at room temperature (the fresher the eggs, the better the results. You may also find egg whites sold in cartons in the dairy section of most supermarkets, but to guarantee a better meringue, use the freshest egg whites possible)
- Gold luster dust (can be found at Michaels or specialty baking shops) for decorating macarons
- Candy thermometer
- Piping bags with ½-inch round piping tips

1. For the Macarons: Combine the almond flour, confectioners' sugar, lemon zest, and salt in a food processor and process until finely ground, 1 to 2 minutes. Sift the mixture into a clean stainless-steel bowl to remove any lumps.
2. Pour the water into a small saucepan and add the superfine sugar. Gently agitate to mix. Using a candy thermometer, cook over medium heat until the sugar syrup forms a soft ball or the thermometer reads 118°C/235°F.
3. While the sugar syrup is cooking, pour half of the egg whites (3 tablespoons plus 2 teaspoons) into a clean bowl of a stand mixer with the whip attachment. Whip the egg whites until they reach stiff peaks. When the sugar syrup reaches the correct temperature, pour the syrup down the side of the bowl, with the mixer still running, to blend with the whipped egg white meringue. Continue to allow the mixture to whip for 4 to 6 minutes, until the meringue is stiff and glossy.
4. Make a well in the almond flour mixture and pour in the remaining 3 tablespoons plus 2 teaspoons egg whites. When the meringue is ready, gently fold it into the almond flour mixture and continue to fold until the batter is smooth and shiny. It should pool slightly in the bowl, like slow-moving lava.
5. Preheat the oven to 325°F.
6. Line a baking sheet with parchment paper.
7. Fit a piping bag with a ½-inch round piping tip. Fill the bag with the batter. Pipe rounds about the size of a quarter and leave about 1 inch between each round. Tap the bottom of the tray, when finished, to release any trapped air. Allow the shells to dry for 20 to 30 minutes, until they've formed a "skin" and are no longer tacky, or sticky to the touch.
8. Bake for 15 to 17 minutes, rotating the pan halfway through the baking period. The macarons are done when they are baked all the way through and the tops of the shells do not slide back and forth when touched. If they are underbaked, they will be mushy on top and not release from the parchment paper easily. If they are overbaked, they will begin to brown.

9. Allow the shells to cool and pair up equal-size shells, lining them up next to each other.

10. Using a clean piping bag and tip, pipe a small amount of the hazelnut ganache into the center of half of the shells. The remaining shells will be used to top the cookies.

11. Using another clean piping bag and tip, on the same side of the filled shell, pipe a ring of the champagne gel around the ganache. Place the partnered shells on top of the filled macaron shells, to make sandwich cookies.

12. Decorate with gold luster dust.

13. Allow the macarons to set in the refrigerator overnight.

14. Remove from the refrigerator 30 minutes before serving, place on a platter, and allow to come to room temperature.

BLUSHING BRIDE AKA PINK GIN & TONIC

YIELD: 8 TO 10 SERVINGS

- 1 750ml bottle Pink Gin (there are so many new brands, but my favorite is made by The Bitter Truth)
- 1 2-liter bottle tonic water
- ¼ cup fresh lime juice
- 2 limes, cut into wedges for garnish

1. Pour the gin, tonic, and lime juice into a pitcher and serve over ice in rocks glasses.

2. Garnish with a lime wedge.

DON'T STAIN MY DRESS AKA WHITE SANGRIA

YIELD: 8 TO 10 SERVINGS

- 1 750ml bottle dry white wine
- ¼ cup brandy
- ¼ cup agave syrup
- 4 lemon slices
- 4 lime slices
- 4 green apple slices
- 1 bunch white grapes
- 1 2-liter bottle club soda

1. In a large pitcher, combine the wine, brandy, and agave syrup. Add ice, the fresh fruit slices, grapes, and club soda.

2. Serve in wineglasses.

ALL-WHITE BAR

Since we do not want any stains
on our precious wedding dress or
handsome tux, I recommend
serving an all-white bar at your
wedding cocktail party: white
wine, sparkling wine (prosecco or
champagne), and sparkling
water *only*.

WALKING FOOD BARS

If you choose to go with an "all-passed" (as in, all the food is passed around) Cocktail Party wedding, then I suggest serving some heartier items, and a great way to do this is with walking snacktivities as shown here with a candy-themed walking bar. Bring the food to the guests, thus keeping the informal party vibe you're going for.

- *Start with a large serving tray with handles. They are widely available online.*

- *Attach heavy ribbon or rope to the handles and then tie around the neck of the server.*

- *Always choose items that only require a plate and a fork or spoon, as you do not want to serve anything this way that needs to be cut. No knives.*

- *Pick something with a hearty base like paella or mac and cheese or a farro salad.*

- *Fill the small plates (you can use disposable or ceramic) with the hearty base.*

- *Next to these plates, fill bowls with toppings:*

  - *For paella: shrimp, chorizo*

  - *For mac and cheese: fried chicken bites, crumbled bacon, chipotle crème, hot sauce*

  - *For a nice veggie option, how 'bout farro, quinoa, or couscous salads: roasted tomatoes, feta cheese, goat cheese, red onions, corn, sliced cucumbers, pancetta, chopped basil or mint, red wine vinegar, and extra-virgin olive oil*

- *Other walking bars: Pretty much any stationary snacktivity we've presented in this book or anything you can think of can be turned into a walking snacktivity: raw bar (seafood), candy, desserts . . .*

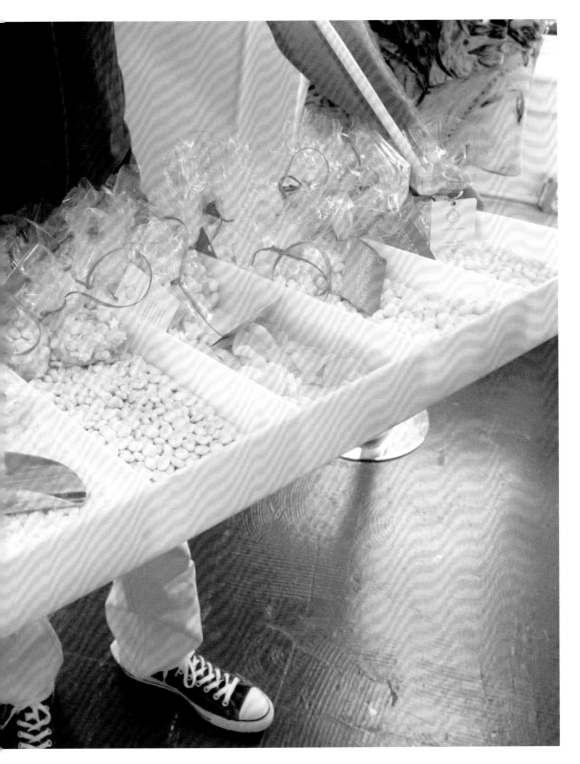

OLD-FASHIONED CHAMPAGNE TOWER

Let's bring it back, shall we? Everything that's old is new again, and the champagne tower is a beautiful way to serve that first toast. In the last year, I have seen a rise in requests for the champagne tower, and I've seen many great ones and a few disasters. Here are a few ways to avoid that second type.

- *Start with a firm and solid base. No wobbly tables for this trick. I love to use a circular table (as shown).*

- *Champagne flutes will not work, so look for the rounded champagne glasses (as shown).*

- *Fill the entire bottom of the table with glasses, leaving about 2 inches clear around the rim of the table.*

- *Start building up like a pyramid, until you are left with one glass on top.*

- *Make sure all the glasses are touching.*

- *Make sure the champagne is properly chilled and all the guests have arrived before you pour. The last thing you want to do is pour too early and have your guests drinking warm champagne.*

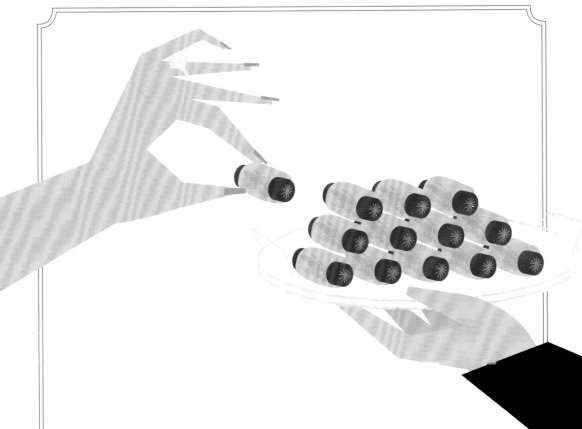

How to Avoid a Wedding Hangover

I've seen it happen one too many times not to alert you. Bride/Groom: YOU MUST EAT!!! You'll say you will, but you won't. This is why I always assign one specific waiter to follow the bride and groom like a neurotic Italian or Jewish mother would. Ask your caterer to assign you your own waiter to make sure that they bring you all the food you've chosen to serve and be ready at all times with something on a tray should you turn around and want to sneak a bite.

Insist that they make you a bridal doggie bag. Trust me: after almost ten hours of smiling and dancing, you'll be so grateful to kick off your shoes and take down some cold pigs in a blanket and mini grilled cheese sandwiches with your new mate!

HAVE NO FEAR, HELP FOR THE ANTIBRIDE IS HERE

I think that, at this point, you know I don't really go for anything too fancy, so just imagine how I—"Caterer to the Stars"—handled my own wedding prep and plans. Here are some highlights:

The Dress: I bought the first dress I tried on and it wasn't all white. It had pink, lavender, and mint-green sparkles. . . . Come to think of it, I looked like a frosted Magnolia Bakery cupcake.

My Hair and Makeup: I did not try out various bridal 'dos and, instead, took my chances at the Sea Barn in Montauk the morning of my wedding, where a lady named Nena curled my hair with an iron from 1981 and used Aqua Net, also from said year, to keep the tight Nellie Olsen–like curls on my head in place (okay, I totally admit it now—the hair was a big mistake). Since I don't normally wear makeup, I didn't plan for that either and my mother and sister emptied out their makeup bags at the Sea Barn Salon and took turns dolling me up.

Our First Dance: The 1981 Christopher Cross hit "Arthur's Theme (Best That You Can Do)" from the film *Arthur*. Yes, our wedding song was the theme from a movie about a drunk bachelor.

The Father-Daughter Dance: Supposed to have been "The Way You Look Tonight" by Frank Sinatra, per the suggestion of the bandleader. However, right before we were set to go, I leaned over and asked him to play "Please Don't Talk About Me When I'm Gone," my Dad's favorite song that he used to sing when he was in the United

States Army Band. It's a really upbeat song and we had a great dance. However, it has *absolutely* no father-daughter corny sentiment with regard to a wedding. At All. It confused the hell out of my guests, but goes down as one of the happiest memories I have with my dad.

Food: I have no idea. . . . Honestly, I think there was a salad and a piece of fish or meat, but I paid little to no attention to that part, as I was too busy getting kisses and my cheeks pinched from the 200 plus Italian relatives that were there. I do remember ordering pizzas to the beach at the after party.

I know . . . I'm a little silly. So, with that in mind, perhaps the suggestions below are a little more you? Still very antibride, but so much fun for everybody, and isn't that the BEST kind of wedding?

Engagement Party Surprise: My favorite type of antibride celebration. I usually recommend this to what I call a Stage 3 antibride. As you know, a lot of time and preparation go into planning a wedding, and if the antibride has a full-time job and will be dealing with opinions from family members and friends for the next six months and the thought of that scares her to death, I suggest a surprise wedding.

Invite guests to your "engagement" party and then, when they arrive, surprise them and get married! The two couples that took my advice and did this had the most memorable and special weddings I have ever seen. They got to have everything their way and not spend months fighting and listening to everyone's "helpful" suggestions.

DRESS: Add some color. You don't have to go crazy; just add a little touch here or there and that will be enough to stand out. One of my favorite antibrides asked all her guests to wear white or shades of white, and she wore a black dress. It was fantastic! FYI . . . Sarah Jessica Parker wore a black wedding dress and had a surprise wedding . . . she is a perfect antibride!

FOOD: Make it about *You*! Take this day as an opportunity to reflect who you and your beloved really are. If a mixed green salad, a piece of filet, and an ordinary slice of cake represent you . . . shame on you! Get creative! During cocktail hour, let your guests learn that your sweetie likes Southern cooking and you love fine French cuisine, or that you met at sleepaway camp and that's why you are having a s'mores bar at dessert. Let the food help tell the story and bring in those little extras that make this day about you. And, drum roll please—this is the perfect opportunity for you to serve an All Passed Menu or an Extended Cocktail Party and let the hors d'oeuvres/small bites tell the story. Start with lighter fare such as tuna tartare or crab cakes and then move into the heartier bites inspired by your sit-down dinner favorites (paella, steakhouse, etc.), then move into mini desserts, and at midnight, serve either lots of mini comfort food favorites or midnight breakfast treats.

BEVERAGES: To save money, offer an all-white bar: white wine, champagne, and a vodka cocktail. It's sure to please all your guests, saves you money, and looks super chic.

MUSIC: DJ, iPod: Surprise your groom and learn an instrument and play one song. Who didn't get the chills during that scene in *Love Actually* when the horn section pops up in the back of the church? Go to your local church and hire the boys' choir.

SEATING: Eliminate place cards and assigned seating (I just felt a very proper bride close this book and reach for one by Martha instead). Your guests will be there for four hours, some traveling across the world to share this special day. Don't make them sit next to your sweet but long-winded Uncle Harold; let them choose with whom they want to sit.

Happy guests = happy party.

I have lots more, trust me, but can't give all my secrets away in the first book. ☺ Just know that I am here for you, My Dear Antibride, and if anything I said made you feel better about your special day, know that you are not alone and the more you think outside of the box, the more wonderful your wedding will be.

MY IMAGINARY BEST FRIEND'S WEDDING

As you may have deduced by now, I wasn't the coolest of kids growing up. One thing I wanted more than anything (besides being allowed to wax my unibrow) was a best friend who really understood me. While I waited patiently for that friend to arrive in physical form, in September 1984, I turned on my television and there she was in full color . . . my best friend had finally appeared, and her name was Samantha Micelli, played by Alyssa Milano.

She was just like me, a tomboy with a protective Italian father; she, too, was out of place with a family from Brooklyn living in Connecticut (me, Brooklyn on Long Island). There was even a crazy grandmother in her house, too. Mine was suffering from Alzheimer's and living in my basement, and while Mona was more with it than my Grandma Mary, it comforted me to see this type of family dynamic existing outside my home. My mother even had the same hair color as Judith Light, '80s frosted blond!

And, as for so many other young girls growing up in the '80s, Alyssa Milano remained my imaginary best friend for years.

As I grew older, a best friend would finally arrive in physical form (Lauren Balkin), but my love for Alyssa Milano remained strong. Anytime her name popped up in a magazine or TV show, I chimed in.

And then one day, almost twenty years later, my office phone rang and it was Colin Cowie's office (which was exciting in itself), telling me there was a celebrity who could not be named at the time, due to confidentiality reasons, who had chosen a photo of our food featured in a wedding magazine and wanted me to cater her special day. At that point, I had no idea that this confidential celebrity was indeed my childhood best friend . . . Alyssa Milano!

When I heard she wanted a family-style, sit-down dinner, it was like she knew my secret, for Alyssa had been part of my family already for so many years, it only made sense that this was the format she would choose.

On the day of her wedding, I came with my A Game ready. I was going to give my imaginary childhood best friend the best wedding she could ever dream of. I had planned, double-planned, triple-planned, even had a plan for my plans, but never did I expect the following event to enter into my plan.

An hour before the ceremony, I made my way from the wedding tent toward the house to get something from my car. As I was walking up the driveway, I glanced toward a bedroom window and saw what I thought may have been my childhood best friend's wedding dress hanging near the window. Now, I have done many incredible weddings and usually grown attached to the bride and groom, but this has never happened. I began sobbing, really sobbing tears of joy and "I can't believe I am doing my imaginary best friend's wedding" elation!

In that exact moment, I took stock and was grateful knowing that the answer to that question my mother used to ask me over and over again during our childhood game became perfectly clear. I was doing what I loved and I was exactly what I wanted to be. I was filled with appreciation for all the people who had helped me find my way. The ones who didn't laugh when I told them my big plans . . . who said, "You can" rather than "You can't." Gratitude for my loving Italian family and equally as loving Italian-Irish husband; my heart exploding with gratitude for every chef, planner, waiter, captain, coat check attendant, and driver who worked so very hard for my company on a daily basis.

Sobbing, I stood frozen in that moment until I suddenly heard my business partner and dearest friend Michele, yelling and shaking me, "What the hell is wrong with you? Get it together! We have a wedding to do!"

And so we did . . . the night was perfect.

Weeks after the wedding, the photos appeared in *People* magazine and I was able to tell everyone who would listen that I'd catered my imaginary best friend's wedding. An old friend from elementary school on Facebook posted, "Mary, I remember you always loved her; must have been a dream come true."

Yes, it was, it really was.

And, to be honest, so is right now that you're actually reading this book! ⋙⋘

With gratitude and love,
Mary

Resources

eBay: Great for all your retro party finds like fondue pots, warming trays, pupu platters, vintage glassware, bar carts, Easy Bake ovens, etc. ebay.com

Etsy: Great for all of the above as well as custom invites and party decorations (including confetti bombs). etsy.com

Eataly: The BEST grocery store in the world and one-stop shopping for your entire party. You can find the OTTO Black truffle honey here and any other amazing Italian delicacy you desire. eataly.com

IKEA: Amazing source for mini glassware, small cocktail party wares, 4-inch bowls, small plates, votive candles, vases. My go-to store for all things party. Ikea.com

HomeGoods: Great for tablecloths, runners, decorative china, drink dispensers, and custom packaged snacks for Cocktail Party noshing. homegoods.com

Crate & Barrel: Great for drink dispensers, mini ice cream scoops, mini muffin pans. crateandbarrel.com

Michaels: Everything you will need to customize those invites, place cards, and other personalized touches to your Cocktail Party. They also have toothpicks, a great baking supply section, and more. michaels.com

Fishs Eddy: Just go . . . you'll get inspired. I want my ashes to be scattered there. fishseddy.com

Grazie Mille!!

Abbe Aronson, PR Goddess, who proved that Abbe (truly) Does It! Abbe, thank you for believing in me, pushing me, and being so hilarious and fun to work with. Without you project-managing this baby, I do not think this book would have ever happened. I am grateful for the many hours you spent organizing, correcting my dyslexic grammar, and dealing with my ADD. You make work fun!

The "Kitchen Angels" in my life who are kind enough to dream alongside me and tell me just how much flour, sugar, or water something needs. MGCE's Executive Chef and the best catering chef in New York City, my "Paisano," Michael Fiore, for all your recipe help and Liana Gebhardt for all the "sweet" inspiration you added to this book. Special thanks to Matthew Wilbur (MGCE Chef de Cuisine), for being so talented and amazing, and to Kirsten Beasley and Eric See for their delicious recipe contributions as well. Big thanks to Barbara Mansfield for testing all the recipes with love and care.

Jason O'Malley, without your incredible talent and hard work, this book would have never been as pretty or special

Adrien Broom for dreaming in the colors that you do!! Honored to have your magic shoot this book, to be your friend, and to watch you fly! To Kristen Meyer for prop styling in the rain and snow and making it feel sunny with all your unique and creative touches. Lari Lang for all your help with the shoot.

Meg Thompson, the sexiest and smartest lit agent on the planet. Thank you for believing in me and giving me the courage to write this book. I am honored to be working with you and hope this is the first of many.

Pamela Cannon at Random House, the *best* in the business. I am humbled that you chose to work with me and hope I made you proud.

Joanna Adler, I will never forget our Woodstock summer and all the time and energy you put into *If You Can't Join 'Em, Serve 'Em*. You are one of a kind and I was very lucky to work with you. Thank you for getting my stories out of me and for being you.

Carla Nikitaidis for being the kindest, most professional, honest, and caring person. Thank you for everything you have done for me. Adore you beyond words.

Martha Frankel for your endless support and for creating the Woodstock Writers Festival.

My MGCE office "family": Samantha Siciliano, Robson Dematos, Tyler Misenheimer, Alison Norby, Jennifer Perlaki, Ilana Shackman, Crystal Warren, and those who have moved on: Tara Littman, Lauren Nemchick, Neji Ramaida, Karen O'Brien, Liana Gebhardt, Beth Belkin, Kiah Drue, Alexandra Scott, Heather Jaffar, Morgan White, Malissa Schwartz, and Fabio Arruda.

All the lovely interns who have come and gone. Hope you had fun.

To the amazing MGCE waitstaff. Without your hard work there would be no party.

To all our loyal clients, especially those who have been around since the hand-glued artichoke card days.

To Colin Cowie for pioneering the event industry. So lucky to have worked with you and grateful to you for believing in me so early in my career.

Frank and Michele Rella for throwing the best Halloween parties ever! and for all your support during the early days and always.

Anne McDermott at Party Rental for many years of loyal dedication to my company and for correcting all my horrible rental order mistakes.

Mrs. Weinberg (my eighth-grade English teacher), who told me that it was okay that I couldn't spell, to keep writing because I was good at it.

Gail Monoco and the Make-A-Wish Foundation of Metro New York Gang. Thanks, Gail, for loving me despite my occasional "desk naps" and for teaching me that "you catch more bees with honey."

Daniel Mattrocce: Thank you for taking a chance on the girl from Long Island with the yellow legal pad and the Susan Lucci shoes. You showed me that professionalism, hard work, and doing what you love the best will take you far. I will forever be grateful to you for helping me find my way and for making *the best* mac and cheese.

Mario Batali: The man who gives gifts that can truly never be repaid. Because you believed in me, I believed in me, and for that I will always be grateful. And to Team MB (Pam, Tess, David, Katie, Cathy, Susan) for being amazing always!

Mickey Drexler for inspiring me to dream big, be authentic, not be afraid to ask questions, and to lead without bullying. The world is so much cooler with you walking around in it! I am truly blessed to call you and Peggy my friends.

To the ladies who inspire me every day: Lydia Fenet, Stefani Masary, Lauren Balkin-Cohen, Chudney Ross, Annie Nugent, Cindy Haliburton, Jennifer Potenza, Keisha Escoffery, Tamara Lang, Lari Lang, Beth Belkin, Barbara Kopple, Adrien Broom, Reyna Mastrosimone, and Grace Potter. Love you, chickies; I am grateful for the gift of your friendship always.

Harry and Lazslo: Love you. You make me so proud.

Michael Lang for sharing the stories of your life adventures with me.

Lee Blumer for sharing your heart and believing in me. I miss you every moment of every day. Thank you for giving us Alex.

Jennifer Perlaki, you are one of a kind. I don't think there is a kinder, sweeter, more professional woman in the world than you! Thanks for growing up with me. You have always been and always will be a star.

Ryan Brown, vice president of MGCE and my dear friend. We've been together almost ten years and I am so honored to still have you by my side. I'd be lost without you and you know it! Thanks for it all.

Michele Pokowicz, president of MGCE, my business partner, and dear friend, and to Carol and Stephen Pokowicz for making you! Never will I meet a more professional, dedicated, caring, and harder-working star than you! I said it when I first met you and I'll say it again, you are the best in the business, and I'm so lucky and so grateful that I get to work and create alongside you. Thanks for allowing me the time to write this book and for making everything better always! I wouldn't want to live in a world without you in it, Lady Boss!

Grandma Mary and Grandpa Charlie, Grandma Lucille and Grandpa Franklin, Grandma Evelyn and Grandpa Salvator, Queenie and Grandpa O'Brien, Yaya and Papua, Uncle Dean, Uncle Frank and Aunt Carol, John and Billy, Christopher, Carrie Anne, Roseanne and Mike, Michelle, Gregory, Aunt T, Uncle Richard, Brian and Francesca, Scott and Carolyn, Gigi, Sophie, Charles and Pammy, Diggy and Hal Levinson, Sam and Pearl Weinberg, and Shirley and Ernie Bruno for being such loving and supportive family and friends. You make the stories of my life that much richer.

Our beautiful family in North Carolina that gave us the greatest gift we will ever know.

My sister Sophie, you are love.

My beautiful sister and best friend, Nanette. You will always be my hero. I love you with my life. And Eugene, the "bestest" brother-in-law on the planet. And your babies: Luke, Cole, and Mia, the greatest blessings I will ever know. You three monkeys have my heart forever.

My parents, Robert and Nancy, who taught me that dreams have no limits, to respect others, to believe in God and miracles, and to love with all my heart. Thank you for my beautiful life.

My Ryan, sometimes love can stop your heart, but yours started mine. You are the best part of me and our journey has no end.

Index

About the Author

MARY GIULIANI is a party and lifestyle expert and owner of Mary Giuliani Catering and Events. She has maintained a loyal client roster that includes J.Crew, *Vogue,* the Rolling Stones, Bradley Cooper, Stella McCartney, Carolina Herrera, HBO, and many more. Mary has appeared on *Today, Good Morning America,* and *Barefoot Contessa* among other national media. In 2013 she partnered with chef Mario Batali on a catering collaboration called MARIObyMary (mariobymary.com). Mary splits her time between New York City's Chelsea neighborhood and Woodstock, New York, with her husband, Ryan, and daughter, Gala.

marygiuliani.com

Find Mary Giuliani Catering & Events on Facebook

@marygiuliani

Instagram.com/mary_giuliani

Party Notes

Party Notes

Party Notes

Party Notes

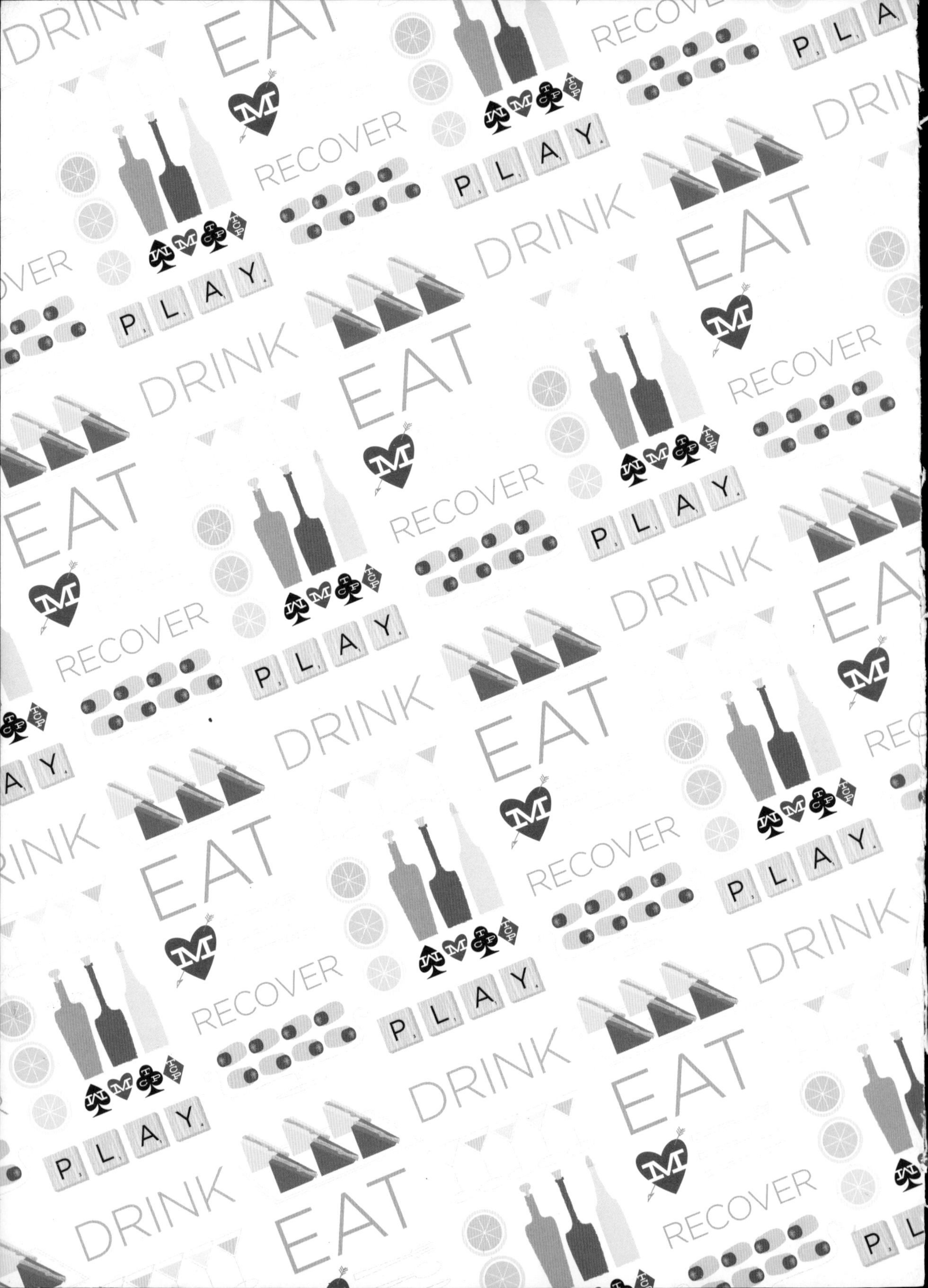
DRINK
EAT
RECOVER
PLAY